Mason Weld

Profits in poultry

Useful and ornamental breeds and their profitable management

Mason Weld

Profits in poultry
Useful and ornamental breeds and their profitable management

ISBN/EAN: 9783337146931

Printed in Europe, USA, Canada, Australia, Japan

Cover: Foto ©Lupo / pixelio.de

More available books at **www.hansebooks.com**

PROFITS IN POULTRY.

USEFUL AND ORNAMENTAL BREEDS,

AND THEIR

PROFITABLE MANAGEMENT.

PROFUSELY ILLUSTRATED.

NEW YORK:
O. JUDD CO., DAVID W. JUDD, Pres't.
751 BROADWAY.
1887.

Entered, according to Act of Congress, in the year 1886, by
DAVID W. JUDD,
In the Office of the Librarian of Congress, at Washington.

PUBLISHERS' PREFACE.

THE experience of poultry-raisers is multifarious. No one person's knowledge covers the whole range of experiences. The present volume is intended to supply a want in poultry literature which can only be compassed by the comparison of the views of many. The results have in some cases been previously chronicled; in others they are now presented for the first time to the public. Through the entire range of this country, extending from the polar circle to the tropics, poultry are now raised with profit. The Publishers believe that no poultry-raiser, whatever his country or latitude, can peruse this volume without both profit and pleasure, while for the novice in poultry-raising it will form a useful and convenient handbook. Among those who have assisted the Publishers in its preparation are T. M. Ferris and M. C. Weld. P. H. Jacobs contributes the chapter on artificial incubation.

CONTENTS.

	PAGE.
PUBLISHER'S PREFACE	3

CHAPTER I.
Poultry Raising... 7

CHAPTER II.
Convenient and Good Poultry Houses.................... 13

CHAPTER III.
Special Purpose Poultry Houses......................... 25

CHAPTER IV.
Poultry House Conveniences............................. 31

CHAPTER V.
Natural Incubation...................................... 46

CHAPTER VI.
Care of Chickens—Coops for them........................ 54

CHAPTER VII.
Artificial Incubation................................... 65

CHAPTER VIII.
Preparing for Market.................................... 80

CHAPTER IX.
Eggs for Market... 86

CHAPTER X.
Caponizing—How it is done.............................. 93

CONTENTS.

CHAPTER XI.
Poultry Keeping as a Business.......................... 98

CHAPTER XII.
Hints about Management................................ 101

CHAPTER XIII.
Some Popular Breeds................................... 121

CHAPTER XIV.
Asiatic Breeds.. 123

CHAPTER XV.
European Breeds....................................... 136

CHAPTER XVI.
American Breeds....................................... 168

CHAPTER XVII.
Diseases of Poultry................................... 178

CHAPTER XVIII.
Parasites upon Poultry................................ 189

CHAPTER XIX.
Raising Turkeys....................................... 198

CHAPTER XX.
Raising Geese... 210

CHAPTER XXI.
Raising Ducks... 218

CHAPTER XXII.
Ornamental Poultry.................................... 235

CHAPTER XXIII.
Theory and Practice................................... 247

INDEX—Alphabetical.................................... 255

PROFITS IN POULTRY.

CHAPTER I.

POULTRY RAISING.

No other business connected with agricultural pursuits, seems so attractive as poultry farming. Even those who fail in the business and retire from it, aver that they are certain they could succeed in a new trial. At the start, the general idea is that the business consists of throwing out corn to a flock of hens with one hand, and gathering eggs with the other. But while this may be true in some cases, it is very different in others. The expert poultry raiser may perhaps meet with no difficulty, and all may go on smoothly, but the novice is in trouble from the first; the eggs are few, and the chicks die. One may easily keep ten or twelve fowls with profit, who could not double or treble this number successfully, because with a large number all the difficulties which arise, such as want of cleanliness, the presence of vermin, impure air, and risk of infection, increase in a much larger ratio than does the number in the flock. But if one has succeeded with a small flock, there is no reason why he should not be able to do so with several flocks, if each is kept in just the same manner as the original one. Afterwards the flocks may be enlarged, but as this is the very point on which most of the younger poultry raisers fail, the greatest caution should be observed in adding to the number of fowls kept in each coop or house, or yard.

THE BEST BREED FOR MARKET PURPOSES.

What follows in this chapter is from E. A. Samuels of Massachusetts: I find it very difficult to answer the question : "Which breed of fowls do you recommend as being the best for market purposes?" for it is almost impossible to lay down as a guide any rule, or name any particular breed, or cross, or variety which will net the best results in *every* market. A great deal depends upon the locality where the breeder is situated, and it also depends upon whether the breeder desires "broilers," or early or late "roasters."

In the Philadelphia, Baltimore and New York markets, as well as among the Paris and London dealers, chickens with white or light skin are preferred to those with yellow skin, and consequently the Dorkings, Black Spanish, Houdans, and other white skinned varieties or their crosses always bring the best prices, and are in the quickest demand, while in the Boston and the other New England cities, and in Chicago, and perhaps some of the other large western cities, where any decided preference has been expressed, the yellow-skinned birds are in the greater demand.

In the Boston markets and hotels a lot of bright, yellow-skinned chickens will always command a better price than will a lot of white-skinned birds, although the two lots may have been fed precisely alike, and be in equally as good condition; this I have proved repeatedly, so that, as I before stated, a great deal depends upon the intended market.

Many persons believe that the color of the chicken's skin is governed largely by the kind of food the birds are provided with; believing that yellow Indian corn will produce a yellow-skinned chick, while wheat or oats will cause the skin to be white. Although there may be some little reason for this belief, I think that it cannot be regarded as of much importance, for a lot of chickens of different varieties, if fed and reared in the same pen, will exhibit all shades of color in the skin from yellow to white. It seems natural to some breeds to secrete a fat that is yellow, while other breeds secrete a fat that has but little tint.

A great deal has been written in regard to the merits of different breeds of fowls, and people are, generally, pretty well acquainted with the characteristics of each, so that it would seem almost an act of supererogation here for me to dwell upon this topic, did not my experience in a measure differ from that of many writers. From extended and careful observation, I have arrived at the following conclusions :

If a breeder intends to raise chickens for the Philadelphia and other first-named series of markets, a cross of Plymouth Rock cock, one year old, on a two-year-old Light Brahma hen, produces the most desirable early "roasters;" a pure-blood Plymouth Rock mating gives the best "broilers" and late "roasters." In fact for my own table I prefer Plymouth Rock chickens, either as broilers or roasters, to all others. Of course, at present, Langshans and Wyandottes are too valuable to be taken into account as table fowls.

Next to the above matings, for the markets named, a cross between a yearling Black-breasted Game and White or Buff Cochin, makes desirable broilers, but not so quick selling as those first named.

In my experience, the principal objection to Plymouth Rocks and their crosses lies in their dark pin-feathers, which abound in the skin of broilers, and are very difficult to be removed, and when they are taken out thoroughly the skin is often badly broken and marred by the picker.

For the Boston and other markets named in the second list, I find that for broilers a cross between a yearling White Leghorn cock, on a two-year-old Light Brahma hen, is by all odds most desirable. The chicks mature very rapidly; they are plump and full-breasted at nine to twelve weeks old; they have a bright, yellow skin, and no dark pin-feathers.

I prefer a two-year-old hen to breed from for the reason that her chickens are larger and more vigorous than are those of a yearling, and they mature much more quickly.

Next in value for broilers in these markets to this cross, in the succession théy are named, are the pure-blood Light Brahma, Plymouth Rock, White or Buff Cochin, and cross of Brown Leghorn on Partridge Cochin, all of the age of from ten to twelve weeks old if hatched in January or February, or nine to eleven weeks old if hatched in March or April, they growing a little more rapidly then than the earlier hatched birds. For early roasters, for these markets, I prefer a cross of Plymouth Rock yearling cock on Light Brahma hen, the latter furnishing the large frame-work on which the blood of the former builds a full-breasted, quick-maturing fine-meated bird. Light Brahma cockerels, nine to twelve months old, make good and marketable roasters, but they are not so profitable to raise as the cross I have named.

MANAGEMENT AND FEED.

As much depends on the management of the chickens, however, as on the characteristics of the different breeds. A good poultryman may, with poor stock, succeed better than would a bad manager with the best of stock.

It is of great importance, in raising chickens, that they should be well supplied with a variety of food. "Short commons" does not pay in chicken raising. The common custom is to keep a dish of "Indian meal dough" mixed up, and three times a day a lot is thrown down to the chickens. If they eat it, well and good; if not, and the chances are they will not, having become tired of one single article of diet set before them day after day, it stands and sours. If a quantity is thus found uneaten, the next meal is likely to be a light one, and the chickens, driven by hunger, finally devour the sour stuff. The result is cholera or some other fatal disease sets in and their owner wonders why his chickens are dying off. In my own practice I find that small quantities of varied food, if given to the chickens often, produce vastly better results than any other method of feeding.

On no account, do I permit young chickens to be fed with Indian meal dough. For the first morning meal I give all my young stock boiled potatoes mashed up fine and mixed with an equal quantity of Indian meal and shorts. I find nothing so good and acceptable as this food, and I use only small unmarketable potatoes; they prove more profitable than anything else I can employ.

I have had many hundreds of chickens at one time in my houses, varying in size from those but a few days old to others large enough for the table, and positively no other article of "soft food" was ever given to them; and I venture to say a more healthy and thrifty lot of chickens could not be found. When, in days gone by, I used to feed to the young stock the traditional "dough," I always counted on losing a large percentage, and the numbers that died from cholera, diarrhœa and kindred diseases, were great. Now a sick chicken is a rarity in my yards. After the potato mash is disposed of I give my chickens all the *fine* cracked corn they will eat up clean. Of course large chickens, those which are ten or twelve weeks old, can be fed with corn coarser cracked, but the young birds want it very fine. In about two hours after the cracked corn is eaten, I give all the wheat screenings the chicken will eat, and in another two hours, some oats. For supper they have all the cracked corn and wheat they can eat. It is of the utmost importance that the young birds should, at the close of the day, have full crops; for the nights in the winter and early spring are long, and as soon as the chickens have digested all their food they stop growing for the time being. I always make it a point to feed them as late in the afternoon as they can see, and as early in the morning.

By the above described system of feeding, the chickens are constantly tempted by a variety of healthy food, and the result is a rapid growth and perfect immunity from disease. If abundance of grass is not accessible to them, young chickens should have fed to them at least one meal a day of grass and clover chopped fine with a pair of scissors. In winter I give my chickens cabbages, throwing in whole heads for the birds to pick at.

CHAPTER II.

CONVENIENT AND GOOD POULTRY HOUSES.

A VERY CHEAP HEN HOUSE.

Experience has proved that twenty fowls, properly housed, provided with suitable food, pure water, clean nest boxes, plenty of dust, lime in some form, and gravel, will return more clear profit than fifty, kept as they generally are upon farms. Suggest a good poultry house to the average farmer, and frequently there arises in his mind the image of an elaborate affair costing one hundred, to one hundred and fifty dollars. Not being able to spare that amount for such a purpose, he goes without, and his poultry, exposed to the inclemencies of the

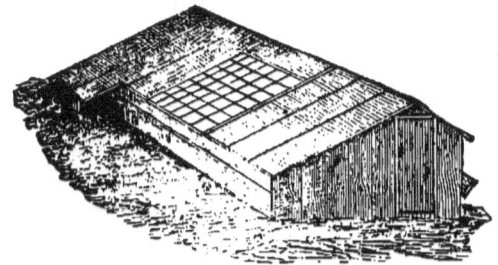

Fig. 1.—A CHEAP HEN HOUSE.

weather, are a dead expense fully two-thirds of the year, eating valuable food constantly and yielding nothing in return. A poultry house large enough to properly shelter twenty fowls can be erected at a very small cost. We give an engraving of one, all the materials of which, with the exception of the sash, cost three dollars and eighty-five cents. The sash was taken from a hot-bed that is used for sprouting sweet potatoes late in the spring. When the sash is required for the hot-bed the season is mild and the opening is covered with boards. This structure is nine feet wide, twelve feet long, and five feet high in the center. The short side of the roof is two feet long, and the long side, which fronts south and comes to within eighteen inches of the ground, is seven feet. At the further end the roof boards extend over an opening made for the fowls to pass in and out. The perches are one foot above the floor and extend along the north side of the interior. The bottom board on that side is hung with hinges so it can be raised, and the droppings under the perches scraped out. The nest boxes are ranged along the low side, the dust box is placed in the sunniest spot, and the feed and water troughs near the door. One pane of glass in the sash is loose so that it may be moved down for ventilation. The floor should be covered with sand when obtainable, if not, with straw, chaff, or other similar material that can be raked out when soiled. The whole interior should be given a coat of fresh lime whitewash at least four times a year, and the perches swabbed with kerosene. Hens kept in this house lay steadily all winter. The poultry house here described is easily cleaned, and answers the purpose nearly as well as one costing twenty times as much.

A WARM FOWL HOUSE.

Eggs in winter are what we all want. To secure them we must have for our hens a warm, snug house, easily kept clean, with provision for dusting, feed, water and exercise. To consider these requirements in the order named, we have first warmth as an important desideratum. Artificial heat has rarely been found profitable, hence we will not consider it. The fowls must depend for their warmth upon the sun, the natural heat of the earth, and the temperature of their own bodies. If we notice a flock of chickens, we shall see that they warm themselves by huddling together, by crowding on their roosts, by sitting flat upon the ground, and by standing or sitting in the sun. We must therefore employ all these ways to secure that warmth, without which we shall have few eggs, with no less or even greater expense for food.

Fowls suffer most from cold at night. In fact, nights are almost always colder than the days, and it is fortunate that by night when it is cold, we have less wind. A poultry house to be warm, must be close and tightly made, yet with good ventilation, for if warm and ill-ventilated, the birds may be suffocated. This has not un-

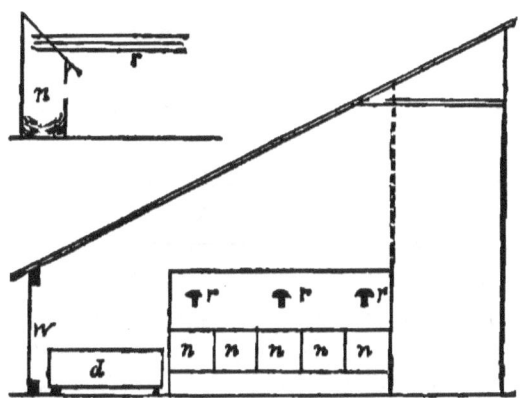

Figs. 2 and 3.—SECTIONS OF ROOSTING ROOM.

frequently occurred. By the accompanying section and plans (figs. 3 and 4), we secure warmth from every source. Too much sunlight is often disadvantageous, hence the low roof without windows. The windows (*w*), admit sunlight upon the floor and dust box. The house is twelve feet square, divided by a partition of boards. This leaves the two apartments each six feet wide. It is intended for less than twenty to thirty adult fowls. The perches (*r*), are five feet long each, so that thirty fowls will be pretty well crowded upon them. The full hight of the house is nine feet, in order to give the roof a good pitch, but within a ceiling is placed at the hight five and a half to six feet. This may be of slats, or plastering lath, placed the width of a lath apart, and in the winter the space above may be filled loosely with straw. Thus, with ventilating doors above, there can be no direct draft upon the fowls. In such a room there will always be a circulation of air. The air warmed by the bodily heat and the breadth of the fowls, rises into the upper part of the room. There is a constant current of cool air flowing down against every window, and this causes a circulation —up through the roosts, down by the window. After a while the air may become charged with carbonic acid gas from the breath of the fowls. This is heavier than the air, hence would, after being chilled by the window, not be likely to rise, but would in part flow off into the other compartment, through the passage for the fowls near the window. The closeness of the quarters for the number of fowls stated, will secure a high temperature at night, provided the walls and roof are reasonably tight, without danger. Perhaps the best way to secure a warm roof is the following: lay first a roof of hemlock boards, laid with the slope; upon these, shingling laths, and shingles. This secures an air space an inch thick under the shingles, in addition to the board roof. So constructed, no rafters would be needed, but one scantling, set edgeways and supported by posts in the middle of each side, and in the partition, to make the roof stiff.

The roosting-room is supplied with a large dust-box, always well filled, and two ranges of nest boxes, with sloping tops, as shown in figure 2. The chickens can not stand on these tops, and being set on each side of the room, they are made to support the roosts, which should not be higher than two feet, or two and a half feet from the floor. The best form of roost is made by taking two straight grained, smooth pine sticks, two inches wide and one inch thick, and nailing them together **T**-fashion.

If the top edges of the cap piece are rounded off by a plane, the result will be a stiff, strong perch, which will not disfigure the breast-bones of fowls, and which will keep their feet warm.

This apartment should be cleaned out every morning. To do this the perches are taken up, cleaned off with a wooden knife or scraper, and set in one corner. The roofs of the nest boxes are cleaned off with the same implement, and after scattering a little of a mixture of road-dust and plaster over the floor, all is swept up and put

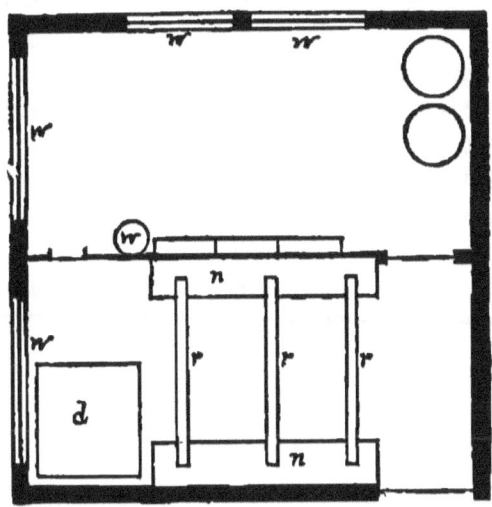

Fig. 4.—PLAN OF FOWL HOUSE.

in a barrel. Then a small layer of dust is scattered over the floor under the roosts, which however are not replaced until evening, or say three or four o'clock, when the last gathering of eggs is made.

We have considered the matter of warmth, and incidentally that of dusting, and in part of cleanliness. The day compartment is as light as we can conveniently make it. It ought to have a cement, or hard clay floor, well pounded down. Cement is preferable. The water fountain (*w*) should be cleaned and filled daily. If there is danger of its freezing, the water may be thrown out as soon as the fowls are on the roosts, and refilled with tepid water at daylight in the winter mornings. Three feed boxes are sufficient, one for soft feed, one for ground oyster shells, and one for ground bone. Grain should be fed upon the floor, and preferably at evening. This brings us to consider the last of our list of requirements, namely, exercise. To secure this, cover the floor with chopped straw to the depth of three inches, and scatter the grain upon this. Feed at such an hour that the chickens will not have time to find it all before it is dark, and this will be an inducement for them to get up early and go to scratching. Some provision of this kind is very important when fowls can not have much range and out-of-door exercise on account of snow and rain. In winter a dry outside run is very important. It is best provided by a long, low, lean-to roof, on the south side of an east and west fence. The sun should, even at noon, reach all the ground under the shed. If such a house as we have indicated, be built against a hillside, somewhat sunken perhaps ; and earth banked up against the sides, except where windows come, will add greatly to its warmth.

CONVENIENT AND CHEAP POULTRY HOUSE.

Those who need a cheap building, and can do the greater part of the work themselves, will find the following plan excellent. The center of the building (see fig. 5), is 10x10 feet, and is six feet to the eaves. The wings are each 8x6x4 feet. Either of the three parts may be built first, and the others may be added from time to time. No posts are used in building it. The sills, 3x4 inches, and 10 feet long, and are mortised and put together in place ; the plates, 3x4 inches, and 10 feet long, are put on the sills ; then eight boards are cut six feet long, four of them with the angle at the top to correspond with the pitch of the roof. These are nailed to the sills, and

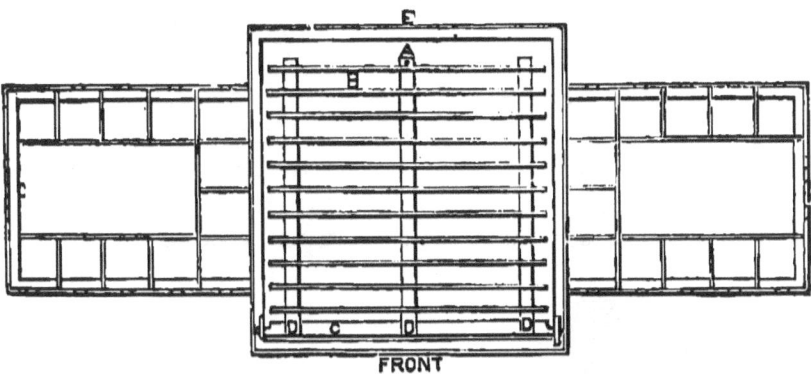

Fig. 5.—GROUND PLAN OF POULTRY HOUSE.

those in front and back nailed to the edges of those on the ends. Then four sticks are cut each five feet six inches long, the plate is raised up, a stick put under it

Fig. 6.—FRONT ELEVATION OF POULTRY HOUSE.

on the sill, in each corner : the boards are then nailed to it, and the frame is raised ; boarded, and battened, and it is strong enough. The roosts are arranged as in figure 5; the piece, *C*, rests on the plates, and is held in place by cleats, and acts as a hinge. The pieces, *D*, are secured to it, and the roosts, *B*, to them. At *A* is a ring bolt, and overhead a hook. When the house is to be cleaned out, the roosts are raised and hooked up, and are six feet high, so there is no trouble in working under them. The door, *E*, is 6x3 feet. In each wing there are two rows of nests, each nest 18x18x12 inches, 12 in a row, 24 in each wing, and 48 in all; the bottom of the lower row is two feet from the ground, and under it are five coops on each side, in each wing, twenty in all, (18x18x20 inches). These are closed inside with slats, and each one is inde-

Fig. 7.—END ELEVATION.

Fig. 8.—SECTION.

pendent, and entered from the outside, as shown in figures 6 and 7. The entrances to the nest-rooms are in the doors, as in figure 7. Figure 8 is an inside view of one of the wings, showing the interior arrangement of one side. The two windows in front, one in each wing, three doors, and twenty-three entrances for the fowls, will give sufficient ventilation, but if more is needed, small doors or windows, 18x18 inches, can be put above the plates, in the ends of the center building. The cupola is not necessary, but it allows the foul air to escape; it costs about a day's work for a handy man, and is built of scraps. The roof need not, of necessity, be shingled.

CHAPTER III.

SPECIAL-PURPOSE POULTRY HOUSES.

A VERY COMPLETE POULTRY HOUSE.

The very complete yet simple plan for a poultry house on the following pages was submitted by Charles H. Colburn, of New Hampshire, in competition for prizes offered by the publishers, and received the highest award. It is built with the windows to the south. Fig. 9, a, is a door eighteen inches square for putting in coal; b is a place for early chickens; c, boxes for oyster shells and ground bone; d, movable coops for hens with chickens. The inside doors are at e, e, e, e; boxes for soft feed at g, g, and bins for grain are at h, h. A scuttle for the droppings is placed at i, in the passage-way, under which is a receiving box, and a track laid to the door j. This door is hung with T-hinges, and opened only for the passage of the box. A ventilating hole is left in the door. The nests for setting hens are at k; lobby for the hens at l, and small ten by twelve-inch openings through the wall for hens to enter the yards, are shown at m. Other similar openings for hens pass from yard to yard are at n. A small coal stove, o, is used to cook feed and for heating rooms in the coldest weather. Lead pipes, p, boxed up and packed with sawdust, run under the floor of the passage-way from the water tank to the end pens, where a faucet is attached and regulated that water will fall into dishes. The windows are at q, nine by twelve-inch glass; each sash is arranged to raise. The roosts, r, are one and a half by three inches, and rounded on the edge. The platform, s, under the roosts, is three feet wide, with a two-inch strip on the front; the whole may be covered with zinc if desired. There are two rows of nests, *t*, under the roosts, made with movable bottoms and sides, and may be taken out and cleaned from the passage-way. There are eight doors opening into the passage-way, that eggs may be gathered without going into the pens. Two long doors (one by seven and a half feet), hung with T-hinges, open upward, through which droppings can be easily removed. A water tank, *u*, holding a few gallons, is boxed up and packed in sawdust. There is a ventila-

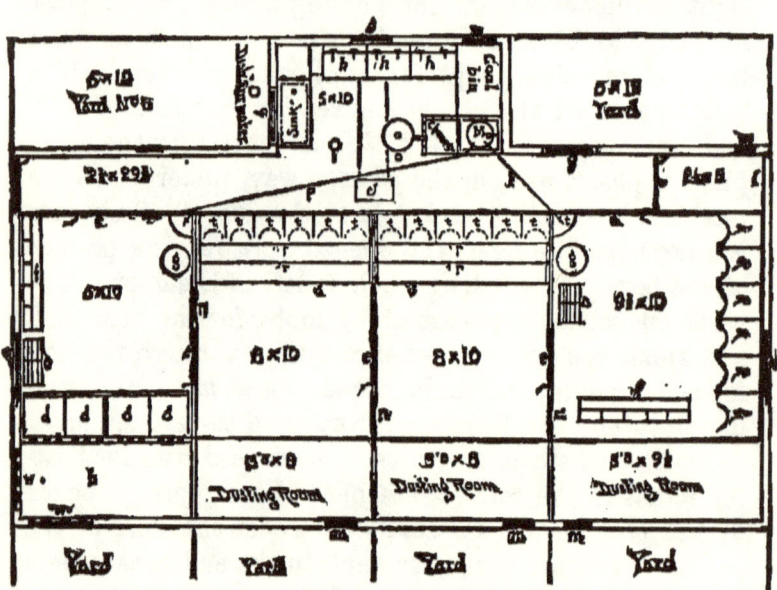

Fig. 9.—PLAN OF THE POULTRY HOUSE.

tor in the center of the roof that can be opened or closed by a cord from the passage-way. A double set of drawers, *v*, for holding eggs, may be made over the grain bins. A lattice door, *w*, is built in the wall for chickens, with a tight door in the outside that can be fastened up or down as desired. Small chickens may be fed from the outside by sliding the window, and from inside by letting down a board over the coops, or by opening a small door in the back of the coop. Over the sink, *x*, is a board (eighteen

SPECIAL-PURPOSE POULTRY HOUSES. 23

by thirty-six inches) with hinges, to be raised up as a side table for holding fowls while being dressed. A cupboard

Fig. 10.—THE SOUTH SIDE OF THE POULTRY HOUSE.

under the sink holds the knives, lantern, etc. At one end of the cupboard is a box for oyster shells and ground bone. A pail is set at y to catch the blood when fowls are killed. Over this pail, screwed into the rafter, is a hook with cord attached, to hang up the poultry by the legs, and a cord with a loop in it and a window weight,

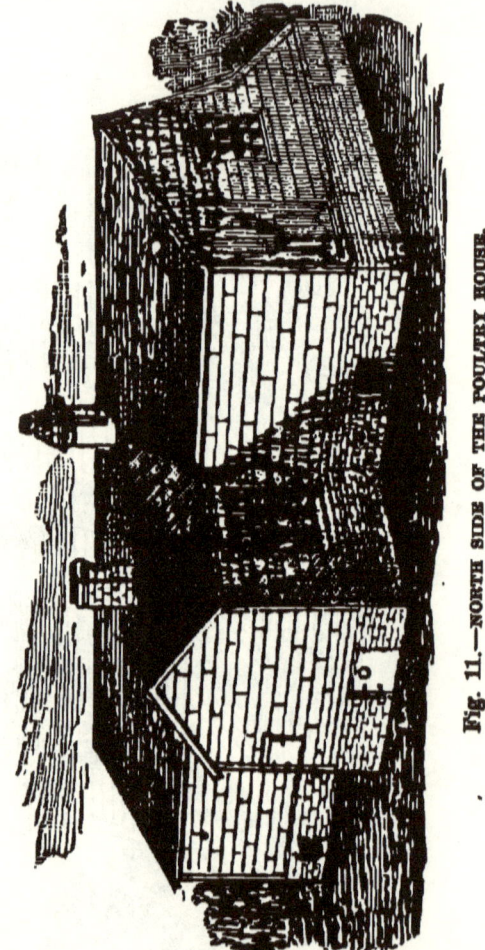

Fig. 11.—NORTH SIDE OF THE POULTRY HOUSE.

to be put over the fowl's neck before being struck with an axe. A small passage under the walk, is for fowls to enter the yard.

This poultry house can be built for $165.70, and when lathed and plastered will cost twenty-five dollars more.

It may be constructed for $130 by having the studding and rafters 22 inches apart, instead of 16 inches, and by setting it on posts and planked up two feet, in place of brick underpinning. The following are the estimates of material:

1 M Square Edge Boards for outside	$12.00
150 ft. Matched Spruce for entry floor	2.25
400 ft. Pine Sheathing for partitions, platforms, and doors	7.20
100 pieces 1¼ by ⅜ Pine for open work of partitions and caps	50
480 Chimney Brick	2.40
Lime and laying brick	2.00
400 Spruce Clap-boards, laid 4 inches to weather	7.00
3¼ M Shingles	7.70
Outside Door and Frame, 2½ by 6½	2.25
8 Windows and Frames, 9 by 13, glass	16.00
4 Sashes over Dusting Room	8.00
30 ft. of Capping	30
Hardware, including zinc, nails, locks, hinges, cords, etc.	10.00
175 ft. Pine Boards for nests, boxes, etc	3.75
1168 ft. Timber	16.25
Labor	20.00
Painting	10.00
4 M Brick	22.00
Lime, Cement, and laying brick	10.00
Iron Sink	1.25
155 ft. Pine Finish for outside	3.10
23 Matched and Grooved Boards over Dusting Room	1.75
Total	$165.70

HALF UNDERGROUND FOWL HOUSE.

The Poultry-House, Fig. 12, is intended to be four feet below the surface of the ground. In this case the bottom should be well drained, at least a foot in depth beneath the wall, and the house must be kept well ventilated, to avoid dampness, which is the most injurious thing possible for fowls. If perfectly dry such a house would be unobjectionable. As to interior arrangements, there should be an entrance as shown at *a*, fig. 13, opening on to a plank extending the whole length of the

Fig. 12.—EXTERIOR OF POULTRY-HOUSE.

building, from which the fowls can reach the roosting poles. Beneath the poles there should be a sloping partition, upon which the droppings may collect and slide down to the plank-walk already mentioned. From this they should be swept off every day, and carried away. To prevent the droppings from clinging to the partition, it should be well dusted every day with dry plaster, road dust, or sifted coal ashes. Beneath the plank walk let the partition extend to the floor, dividing the house into two apartments. At the front of the house a row of nest boxes, supported by braces, as seen at *b*, should be made. The rear partition may be devoted to hatching and rearing chickens, a door at the further end of it opening into the front apartment. This would make an excellent poultry house for a village lot, being cheap, plain, and including many conveniences under one roof. The sash in front sloping to the south, would keep the house

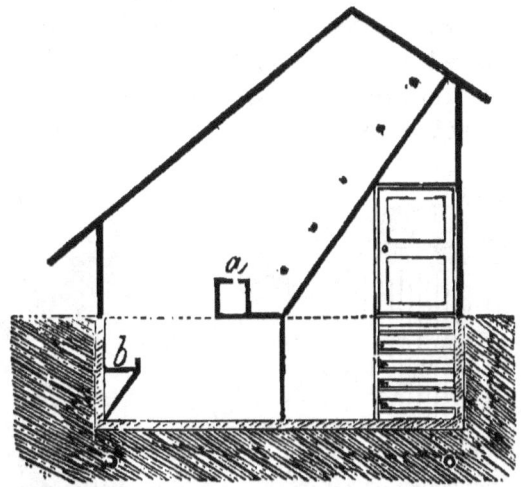

Fig. 13.—SECTION OF POULTRY HOUSE.

warm during winter, and with proper care to feed the fowls well, and keep the house perfectly clean, eggs might reasonably be expected all the winter.

PORTABLE POULTRY-HOUSE.

A movable poultry-house is by no means novel, it having been described and used years ago. Geyelin described one which was used in grain fields in France to gather the scattered grain after harvest. This was constructed something like one of those vans used in transporting animals kept in traveling menageries. It was 20 feet long, about 7 feet wide, and the same in height.

28   PROFITS IN POULTRY.

A set of steps was fixed at one end for the fowls to enter and leave, and nest-boxes and roosts were provided within. Several of these houses were drawn to the field, and one of them was furnished with a small apartment for the keeper who attended to the fowls. A large number of fowls could be accommodated in one of these houses, as they were intended to be cleaned daily, and the droppings scattered upon the ground around them as they were moved from place to place each day.

An excellent house of this kind was designed by R.

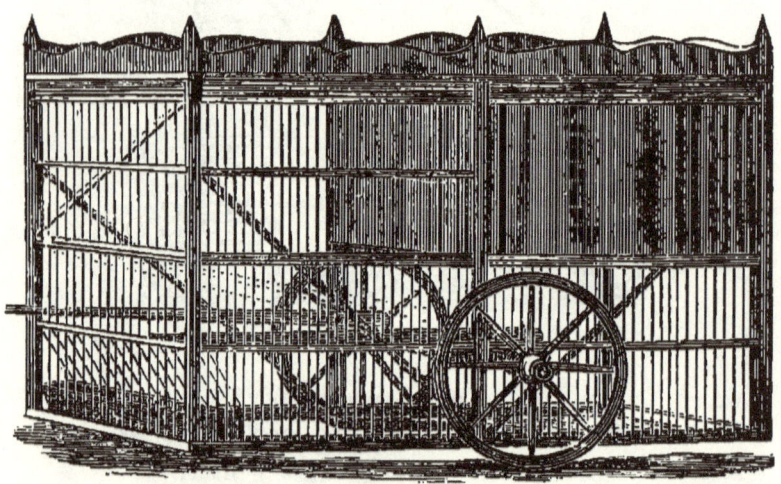

Fig. 14.

Sproule of Pennsylvania, and a view of it is given in figure 14. It is of wood, and as will be seen, is mounted upon an axle and a pair of wheels. By means of a pair of levers, raised to the position shown by the dotted lines, the house is lifted, and made to rest wholly upon the wheels, so that it can be moved from place to place as desired. Figure 15 shows the ground plan, with the boxes for feed, water, and gravel. These are secured to the sills and are kept clean by a sloping cover of small rods. The house is 10 feet long by 5 feet wide, and as high as may be necessary. The nest boxes, 16 inches square and 4 inches deep, are secured to the upper corners of the enclosure, a small door being provided for reaching the eggs. The roosting poles are so arranged that the fowls can easily climb from one to the other. The enclosure is

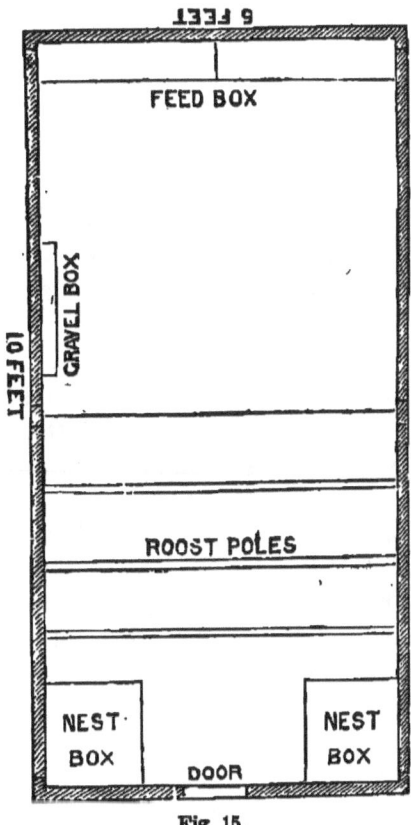

Fig. 15.

made of oak rods and rails which are bored to receive the rods. Any cheaper method of construction may be used.

The size of the house may be 5x10, or 4x8 feet, and 5 feet high to the eaves. The sills are made of 1¼x3 inch stuff, laid flat down, halved together at the corners, and nails driven through upward into the ends of the posts. The corner posts are 3x3 inches, the middle ones are 3x4 inches. Each is properly mortised to receive the rails of the open sections. A light cornice, or a $2\frac{1}{2}$-inch band, is securely nailed around the top, a little above the eaves, leaving sufficient room for the roof boards to pass under between the band and the upper rail. To the back side of this band is nailed the balustrade, each piece having its ends toe-nailed to the posts. A light ridge pole is attached at each end to the balustrade near the top, which forms a double-pitch flat roof. This is made of one thickness of $\frac{3}{8}$-inch boards, the same as the enclosed sides. The upper section at the end, over the feed trough, is hung with hinges for a door through which to place feed, etc. The levers have their fulcrum ends resting on the axle, and are bolted on it. About 12 inches from it, and opposite to it, and through the middle posts, are pivot bolts, on which the weight of the house hangs when the levers are pressed down. Narrow strips are used as braces for stiffening the frame lengthwise, which are placed inside, also bits of hoop iron should be used about the corners to strengthen the joints. With these appliances and proper tools, any skillful mechanic can complete the job. Its weight is about 300 pounds, and the house affords room for keeping from 12 to 24 fowls through the season. The advantages of such a house are that the fowls are under perfect control, and are kept quite as healthy as when running at large. Every morning when the house is moved, there is provided a clean, fresh apartment, with fresh earth and grass. Fowls become thoroughly domesticated by being thus treated. Those that are inclined to sit, are put outside; they will hang about and make an effort to get in, and the desire to sit soon passes away. The manure is all saved to the best advantage, being applied at once.

CHAPTER IV.

POULTRY-HOUSE CONVENIENCES.

Anything that will add to the ease of management of the poultry-yard is gladly welcomed. The practice among farmers of letting their poultry roost about the farm buildings upon harrows, plows, wagons, and farm machinery is growing less prevalent each year, as many of them are building suitable poultry-houses.

PERCHES, ETC.

At figure 16 is shown a neat and handy arrangement of perches; *r, r, r,* are scantling, eight feet in

Fig. 16.

length, two inches thick, and three inches wide, made of some tough, light wood. The upper ends are hinged to the side of the building, four feet apart, and are con-

(31)

nected by means of roosts or perches made of octagonal strips nailed fast to the supports. Perches should be placed about eighteen inches apart. At any time when it is desired to gather up the droppings, the end of the frame-work is raised and fastened to the ceiling or roof by a hook at *n*, the whole arrangement being up out of the way for thorough cleaning. At the corner of the building, opposite the roost, is placed a box, *p*, containing ashes, road-dust, etc., that the fowls may dust themselves. The box should be two feet square and about one foot in height, and should be kept half filled with dusting material, both summer and winter. In the corner is placed a box, *e*, and should contain a supply of gravel and broken oyster-shells. The foregoing conveniences cost but little and will prove valuable additions to any poultry-house.

LOW ROOSTS.

For the large fowls low roosts should be used, as they cannot reach high ones without a ladder, and in dropping from them are very apt to injure themselves. A

Fig. 17.

roosting-frame, made for Asiatic fowls, is shown at Fig. 17. It is made of chestnut strips two inches square, with the edges of the upper part rounded off to make them easy to the feet of the fowls. Three of these strips are fastened to frames made of the same material for supports. The whole is fastened to the wall by rings fixed in staples, so that it can be turned up and held against the wall by a hook. It is twelve feet long, three feet wide, and should stand eight inches from the wall and about one foot from the floor.

STOVE FOR A POULTRY-HOUSE.

A simple and safe method of warming a poultry-house in winter is as follows: With a few bricks and common mortar build a box five feet long and two and one-half feet wide, leaving an open space in the front about a foot wide. Lay upon this wall, when fourteen inches high, so as to cover the space within the wall except about six inches at the rear end, a plate of sheet-iron. Build up the wall a foot above the iron and then build in another plate of iron, covering the space inclosed all but a few inches at the front. Then turn an arch over the top and leave a hole at the end for a stove-pipe. A small fire made in the bottom at the front will then heat this stove very moderately; the heat passing back and forth, will warm the whole just sufficient to make the fowls comfortable, and there will be no danger of injury to their feet by flying up upon the top, as it will never be hot if a moderate fire only is kept. The stove will be perfectly safe, and may be closed by a few loose bricks laid up in front, through which sufficient air will pass to keep the fire burning slowly. Ordinarily a fire need only be made at night during the coldest weather.

NEST-BOXES.

Many farmers and other persons who keep poultry fail to provide nests for their hens, and then grumble because they seek their nests about and under the farm buildings in fence corners, under brush-heaps, and various out-of-the-way places. If clean boxes, provided with straw or other nesting material, had been put up at convenient points, the hens would have used them and would not "steal" their nests. A very good size for a nest-box is little more than one foot square and nine or ten inches in depth. They should be well made; and if planed and painted, all the better. Apply kerosene freely to the inside, where the boards are nailed together. This should be applied early in spring, and again about the first of July; it will kill hen-lice and also prevent their getting a foothold about the boxes.

Fig. 18.

Nest-boxes should never be permanently attached to buildings, but placed upon a floor, or hung upon the side of a hennery or other convenient place for both fowls and attendant. An excellent plan for thus securing the boxes is shown in Fig. 18. At one side of the box, near the top, is bored an inch hole, through which a wooden or iron pin driven in the side of the building passes loosely. Considerable annoyance is often experienced by laying hens interfering with those that are sitting; often a whole sitting of eggs is broken. This trouble is readily avoided by those who have a poultry-house with two rooms, by the use of sliding boxes, as shown in Fig. 19. A hole is cut through the partition about two feet from the floor, to the bottom of which is firmly nailed a shelf or platform, *e, e*, about two feet in length and nearly one foot in width. Upon this board rest the nest-boxes, made so that they can be easily slid back and forth. The ends are made one inch higher than the

Fig. 19.

sides, that they may not slide clear through or fall down. At *b* one box is shown pulled out in the room, while at *a* the box is seen pushed through into the adjoining room. As fast as the hens manifest a desire to sit, they may be furnished with eggs and put in the sitting-room, in which laying fowls are not allowed. As all do not have poultry-houses, a box similar to the one shown in Fig. 20 may be adopted. A light frame-work of lath is placed over the box before moving.

Fig. 20.

A SET OF NEST-BOXES,

made without nails, which can be quickly taken apart for packing away, whitewashing, etc., may be made of any size to suit. The top and bottom boards have tenons on the ends passing through mortises in the endboards, and held in place by wooden pins, as shown in the accompanying engraving, Fig. 21. The top and bottom boards have half-inch holes bored through them, which receive pins that pass into the corresponding

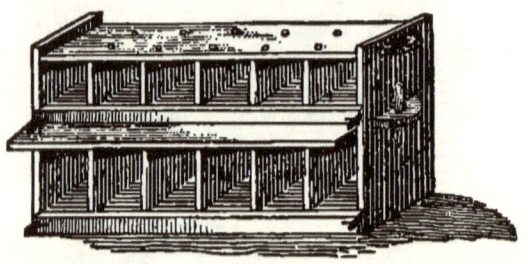

Fig. 21.

holes bored in the edges of the partition boards. As these partition pieces are all alike, they are easily put in place. There is a bar or step along the front of the nests to prevent any eggs from falling out; the bottom board of the upper tier may extend forward for a few inches to serve as a place upon which the fowls may alight.

A NEST FOR EGG-EATING HENS.

In the winter season hens frequently acquire the habit of eating eggs. Sometimes this vice becomes so confirmed that several hens may be seen waiting for another one to leave her nest, or to even drive her off, so that they may pounce upon the egg, the one that drops it being among the first to break it. In this state of affairs there is no remedy except to find some method of protecting the egg from the depredators. The easiest way of doing this is to contrive a nest in which the egg will

POULTRY-HOUSE CONVENIENCES. 37

drop out of reach. Such a nest is shown in the engraving. It consists of a box with two sloping floors; one of these being depressed below the other sufficiently to make a space through which the egg can roll down out of the way. An extension of the box with a lid affords a means by which the eggs can be removed. Upon the bottom board of the nest a wooden or other nest egg is

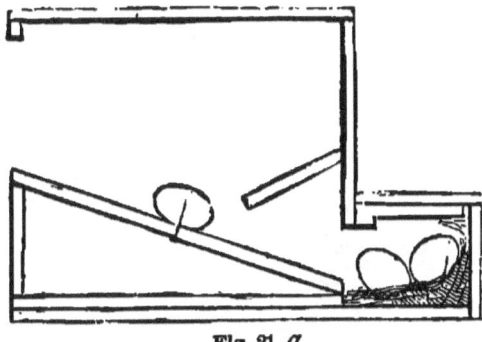

Fig. 21. a

fastened by a screw or by cement. The sloping floors may be covered with some coarse carpet or cloth, upon which it is well to quilt some straw or hay, and the bottom floor should be packed with chaff or moss, upon which the eggs may roll without danger of breaking. If the eggs do not roll down at once, they will be pushed down by the first attempt of a hen to pick at them.

A BARREL HEN'S NEST.

A hen's nest made of a whole barrel is vastly better than one in which the head is knocked out, and the hen is obliged to jump down from the top into her nest, and thus break the eggs. Two staves are cut through immediately above the hoops, and again eight inches above the first cut, the pieces cut out, leaving a hole large enough for the convenience of the hen. Barrels thus arranged are placed in quiet corners, where hens love to seclude themselves, and straw or other material is supplied for the nest.

WIRE NEST.

Figure 22 is an illustration of a good nest, which may be kept free from vermin. It is made of wire, or a similar one may be woven of willows or splints by any ingenious boy. A round piece of wood is fastened to the

Fig. 22.

front for the hen to alight upon, iron or wire hooks are fastened to it, by which it may be hung upon nails driven in the wall, and a piece of shingle planed smooth is fastened to the front, upon which the date when the hen

POULTRY-HOUSE CONVENIENCES. 39

commenced to sit may be written. When a wire nest needs cleaning, it is laid on the ground in the yard, the straw set on fire, and after that is consumed there will be no vermin left to infest the nest. A basket-nest may be drenched with boiling water and purified.

A LOCKED NEST-BOX.

It frequently happens that a nest-box that will lock up is desired. Such a box may be made 3 feet square and 18 inches deep, which will be large enough for two nests. The door is at *a*. At *b* is a partition extending half through the box, and at the inside of this are two

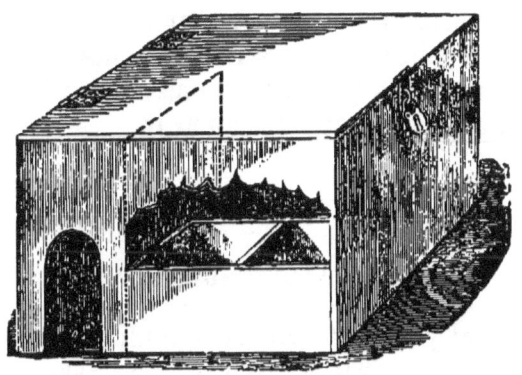

Fig. 23.

nests about 8 inches deep, 16 inches long, and 12 inches wide. These are seen through the side of the box, which is partly removed for this purpose. For small breeds of poultry the box may be made considerably smaller. Such a retired nest as this exactly meets the instincts of the hen, and it becomes very acceptable to her.

TIDY NESTS.

Hens often get the habit of sitting on the edge of their nests, and this results in the defilement of the nests and prevents other hens using them. A roller may be arranged at the front so that the fowls cannot roost upon

Fig. 24.

it, nor stand on it to fight other hens from them. The end partitions are raised 2 inches at the front above the others, and a roller or 8-sided rod, 2 inches thick, is fastened with a wooden pin at each end so that it will turn easily and a hen cannot roost upon it.

PNEUMATIC FOUNTAIN.

To prevent young chicks from fouling the water in the saucers in which it is given to them, take a common fruit can, remove the top, and cut or file but one (and that a triangular) notch, only $\frac{1}{4}$ inch high for a saucer or pan in which water will stand $\frac{3}{4}$ to 1 inch deep, as indicated in the engraving Fig. 25. Fill the can with water, place the saucer on top, and quickly reverse it, and you have a "pneumatic" fountain holding about one quart, which the chickens cannot foul. As the water is drunk or evaporates, more runs out of the can, keeping the saucer always full to the height of the notch.

FEED-TROUGH.

A device for keeping feed-troughs free from dirt, rain, or snow, is shown at figure 26. Supports are attached

Fig. 25.

to the trough, and extend equally above it, as at *E*, *E*, *H*, *H*, and should hold the trough six inches above the ground. When the trough is not in use, it may be tilted

Fig. 26.

over so that it will be kept free from water, or rubbish, and always be in a proper condition whenever needed for use.

WINTER FOUNTAIN.

Poultry sometimes suffer greatly in winter through having their water supply cut off by freezing. There is some difficulty in keeping them constantly supplied with water in severe weather, but it can be done if one appreciates the necessity. A method is here illustrated which has proved of great value. A cask or flour-barrel is sawed in two, and one half used as the covering to the water-jug. An earthen jug is so fastened into the half-barrel by means of cross-pieces that its mouth will come near the bottom of the tub, upon one side—a piece of a stave being

Fig. 27.

removed at that point. The space around the jug is filled with fermenting horse-manure, and slats are nailed across when the "fountain" is ready for use. Fill the jug with water and cork it; then invert the tub, bringing the mouth of the jug over a basin, as shown in the engraving. When the cork is withdrawn the water will flow until the mouth of the jug is covered; it will then cease, and as the water is used, more will come from the jug, and so on, forming a continuous self-acting fountain. Such a contrivance will keep the water from freezing, except in the coldest winter weather. The jug should be emptied at night.

POULTRY-HOUSE CONVENIENCES. 43

FOLDING SHIPPING-CRATE.

On farms, where chickens have full run of the yards, they pick up a great deal of food which would otherwise be wasted, and the cost of raising a limited number is comparatively small; but where they must be fed with grain, the profits are reduced to a fraction, and a very small fraction if they are sold to the storekeeper for "trade." One of the chief reasons why more farmers do not ship their own poultry is the lack of suitable shipping-crates. Express companies charge for *weight*, and unless the

Fig. 28.

crates are light and well made, they object to returning them free. Poultry sells better in crates that are light, handsome, and airy.

An excellent folding-crate invented and used by Fred Grundy is thus described: The crate is exactly square. Figure 28 shows two sides and the bottom, or floor, as they are made and put together. Figure 29 shows the crate empty and folded, also the top, or cover, with its trap-door. The entire frame-work is of any tough wood —ash is best—one and a half to two inches square, according to size of crate. The bottom is half-inch pine. The wire used is common fence wire. The sides (Fig. 28) are hinged to the bottom, or floor, and when folded lie flat on the bottom. On the top of the side, two pins, *a, a*, iron or wood, fit into holes in frame of the cover. The sides are hinged to pieces which are screwed to the bottom, and when folded lie up on the sides. Through

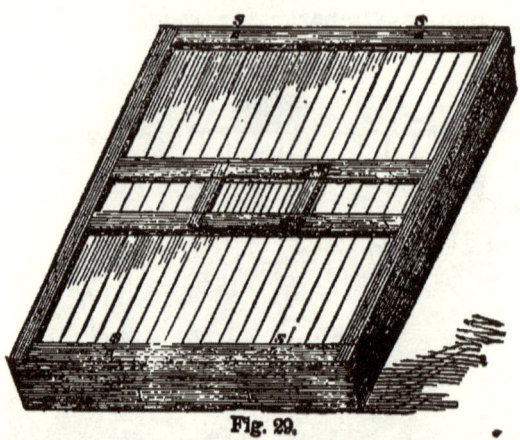

Fig. 29.

the top of the sides are two three-sixteenth-inch holes, *c, c*, into which bolts of the same size are passed, and, entering holes *s, s*, in the cover, hold it down. When the crate is folded these bolts are withdrawn from the holes *c, c*, and passed through the holes *e, e*, in the bottom piece of the same side, and then through holes in cover, and hold the whole crate solid and flat for shipping. Thumb-nuts should be put on these bolts, requiring no wrench.

The crate can be made of any size desired. A crate holding three to five dozen chickens is usually large enough. In shipping long distances care should be taken

POULTRY-HOUSE CONVENIENCES. 45

to not crowd the birds. Give plenty of room and it will pay in the end. Where the distance is short, ten or fifteen hours' travel, they will not hurt in this crate if crowded considerably, as they cannot become heated. When well made of good, seasoned wood, this crate will stand a large number of trips. It should be well washed after each shipment. The wood should be well oiled, but not painted. If thought desirable, the wires on the cover may be braced in one or two places with binding wire. Fasten one end to the frame, wrap it twice around each wire, and fasten to opposite side of frame.

CHAPTER V.

NATURAL INCUBATION

Although, in our opinion, there is greater skill required in caring for the little chicks than in getting them out well, a good deal of the success of the poultry crop depends upon the management of the hens while sitting. Those that steal their nests and follow their own instincts do very well if they are not disturbed, but frequently they get frightened or robbed, and the eggs are lost. As a rule, it is better to have all the sitting birds completely under your control, and make them follow your will rather than their own instincts. With a well-arranged poultry-house it takes but a little time daily to have all the birds come off for food and exercise. But without this we can manage to make the sitters regular in their habits. The best plan, usually, is to set the hens near together in a sheltered spot in boxes or barrels that we can cover, and thus perfectly protect them against enemies, and at the same time compel them to sit until the box is uncovered. Wherever they may lay, when they want to sit, remove them to a shed in an inclosed yard, by night, and put them securely upon a nest full of eggs. Every day about twelve o'clock remove the covers, and carefully take the hens from their nests for food and water. In pleasant weather they take from half to three-quarters of an hour to scratch in the dirt and take their dust-bath. Most of them return to their nests voluntarily before the time is up. Occasionally a bird will take to the wrong nest. It takes but a few minutes to see every bird in her place, and make her secure for the next twenty-four hours. As the hatching-time approaches, dip the eggs in tepid water every day to keep the pores open, and to facilitate the hatching. This moistening of the eggs will be found of special service in the hatching of the eggs of water-fowls set under hens. Following this method, good success with sitting hens is almost certain.

The selection of the eggs for hatching is an important matter. Some of our leading Asiatic fanciers make it a point to select eggs which have a particular cast of color. They claim that dark mahogany color in the shell of Brahma eggs alone indicates their absolute purity. While there are others of equal note as breeders who say it is all nonsense to regard the color of eggs that are deemed fit or unfit for hatching. But it is well, however, to look to shape and size, for it is clearly demonstrated that the regular, medium, well-formed oval eggs without extreme length, very small or very large ends, without wrinkles or furrows of any kind, are the best for hatching.

It is important, too, in the selection of eggs, to look to size. A happy medium must be secured in this as well as in some other things. In size they should be neither too large nor too small for the variety. When eggs of any kind are over-sized, they are usually double-yolked, and are, therefore, useless for hatching. ' And when they are under-sized, they are not so good as the average. Select from your best layers smooth, hard-surfaced eggs, without indentations, and of fair medium dimensions and proportions.

EGG-TESTERS.

A bad egg is never welcome, and any simple device that will quickly and satisfactorily detect the quality of an egg is important. A very simple method is shown in

Fig. 30. The egg is so held that the hand cuts off all direct rays of light from the eye, except those passing through the egg. The egg may be held toward the sun, or, better, toward the light from a lighted candle or lamp in a dark room. Egg-testers are made in which more than one egg may be examined at once. A small box, either of wood or pasteboard, is used, with a number of "egg-holes" cut in the cover. A mirror is placed within, set at a slant towards one side of the box, which is cut away for observation. If the interior of the box is painted black, the effect will be better. The quality of the eggs is determined by their degree of clearness. A fresh egg shows a clear, reddish, translucent light; an egg fit, perhaps, for cooking, but not for hatching, a less clear light.

Fig. 30.

The accompanying engraving (Fig. 31) represents a contrivance for testing the freshness or fertility of eggs, useful in the household or to the poultry-fancier. It consists of a small handle, with a cup in the end of it; around the cup is fastened a frame of sheet-tin or stiff card-board. This frame has a hole in the center, of the shape and size of an egg, and a strip of black ribbon or cloth is fastened around the frame, projecting a little beyond the inner edge. To test the egg, it is placed in the cup, so as to fill

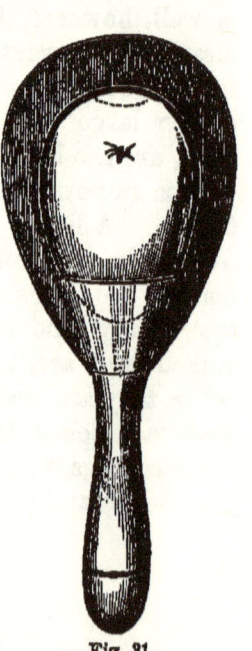

Fig. 31.

the space in the center of the frame, the edge of the black cloth or ribbon fitting close to the shell. When the egg is held close to a bright light, the light passes through the egg, and shows a fresh or infertile one to be perfectly clear, while a fertile one that has been sat upon, or that has been in the incubator two days, will show the embryo, as in the engraving, as a dark cloudy spot. Infertile eggs may then be taken from the nest or from the incubator on the third to the fifth day.

CARE OF SITTING HENS.

March is the month to set hens, for the earlier after this they are set, the better the chicks will prove. Of course every hen has been set that would stick to her nest during the past month; but as hens must lay out their clutches before the sitting fever takes possession of them, the larger number will not be ready for the nest before this month. Sell none but surplus eggs now, but crowd the hens by setting all that can be relied upon. When it comes to finding them all nests, much discretion is needed, that confusion does not cause trouble and loss. Of course, the simplest way to set them is in rows in the hen-house; but the hens will not all remember their own nests, and will crowd two or three on one nest, leaving their own eggs to become cold and perish. It is advisable to set the hens in different rooms and apart from one another; but if the nest rows must be used, then there must be careful watchfulness. A good rule is to keep the windows well darkened, so that the hens will not be tempted to leave their nests until noon. When you give the other chickens their noonday meal, and while they are feeding, go into the hen-house, take all the sitting hens off the nests, and make them go out to feed. While they are out, clear the nests of broken eggs, dirt, and feathers, loosen up the straw a little, and dust Persian insect-powder over the eggs. Now comes the critical time. Do not forget what you have done, and do not trust the hens, but within half an hour be sure to return, and see that each is on her own proper nest, or you will have trouble every time they come off. Hens are creatures of habit, and a little training goes a great way with them. If they can be made to keep the same nest three or four days, there will be little danger that they will make any mistake about it for the remainder of the time. That will save you the trouble of moving them, but not the responsibility of seeing that they return promptly to their nests after feeding. When all is right, darken the sitting-room again and leave them until the next day at feeding-time.

SECURE LAYING AND SITTING BOX FOR HENS.

There have been several devices, some of them patented, for accomplishing this end, which we here show how to do by a simple, home-made contrivance. Take or make a box three feet long by two feet wide (a, a). Take off one side, as shown in figure 32; tack on two cleats. and fit in a partition (d). Take out the partition, and cut a square hole, a little more than a foot square, near one end, and a notch an inch wide and six inches long on the opposite end. Make an opening for the hen to enter by (b), in the end of the box above the partition, and at the point where the notch is cut. The partition d forms the floor of the laying and sitting room. A box a foot square and eight inches deep is made to fit loosely in the opening in the floor. This is the nest, e. It

NATURAL INCUBATION.   51

is balanced on a hard-wood edge, upon the end of a broad lever, which works upon another edge of hardwood affixed to the bottom. A weight, h, placed near the end of the lever, counterbalances the nest as may be necessary, and a tin plate, g, attached to the end of the lever will rise and close the opening b, as a door, when the weight of the hen causes the nest to descend. The entire side, which is absent in the diagram, should be fastened on by screws so as to be easily removed, or attached by hinges to the bottom, so as to give access to the working parts. The sides of the nest must be

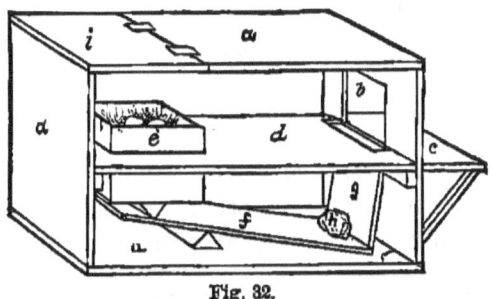

Fig. 32.

greased, and of course the tin door must move up and down without any catching. The counterbalancing of the nest should be so adjusted that the weight of sixteen average-sized eggs, say two pounds and a half, will bring it down. No laying hen weighs less than this, except Bantams, and perhaps some of the Hamburgs. So whenever a hen is on the nest the door will be closed. When she leaves it, the door will open. The advantages are that only one hen will occupy the nest at a time, and fighting over the eggs and breakage are thus prevented. Then, when a hen is set and is likely to be disturbed, the weight may be entirely removed, in which case the door will remain closed, whether she is upon or off the eggs. She may be let out towards evening, daily, after the other hens have laid, or food and water may be placed for her on the floor. In this case, a pane of seven by nine glass ought to be inserted in the top, or on the fixed side. At hatching-time she should be shut in until she brings off her brood. It is, moreover, important that a portion of the top (i) should be removable, or hinged on so that an attendant may have access to the interior at any time. Access to the nest by egg-eating dogs is by this method entirely prevented, unless the dogs are very small, in which case a board a little wider than the door, placed six inches in front of it, and nailed firmly both at top and bottom, will exclude even them.

A BROODING-PEN FOR HENS.

We have for several years used enclosed brooding-pens for hens with much satisfaction. Success with poultry depends wholly upon the convenient and effective man-

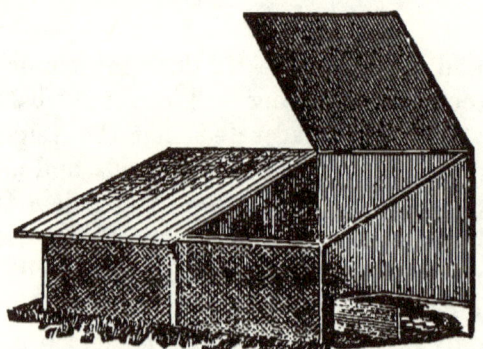

Fig. 33.—BROODING-PEN.

agement of the brood hens and the chicks. When hens cannot help it, they will do as their owners wish, and there are then peace and comfort and prosperity in the poultry-house. These pens are built around a part of the poultry-house, kept specially for the sitting hens. Each one is four by four, and three feet high; it has a hinged lid, which can be thrown back against the wall when it is desired, for attendance upon the hen. The front is covered with wire netting. The nest, shown by the removal of one side of a pen, is a box about sixteen inches square open in the front, and having a very low piece to keep the nest in it, and to permit the hen to step in and out. When it is necessary, the nest is closed by placing a piece of board in front of it. This is done for a day or two when the hen is restless, after having been put in the nest. When she is settled down, the board is removed. Each pen is supplied with a feeding-dish and water-cup, and is littered with sawdust. It is attended to every evening by lamp-light; the feed and water are renewed, and the droppings are removed, a pail and small shovel being kept in the house for this purpose. A pail of water and another of feed are carried to the house every evening. The hens are thus kept undisturbed during the day, although they are visited regularly to see that all is right. Each hen is separate and cannot see the others, and, the house being partly darkened and kept warm, the hens are quiet and comfortable, and mind their business satisfactorily.

CHAPTER VI.

CARE OF CHICKS—COOPS FOR THEM.

The foundation of the various poultry diseases is generally laid while the young chicks are in the coops. There they are crowded in a confined place, which is frequently damp and unclean. They are shut up close at night in these impure quarters, or they are allowed to

Fig. 34.

go out early in the morning, while the grass is wet with dew, and becomed chilled. Some die and some survive, to live unhealthily and die finally of roup or cholera. To prevent these troubles, the chickens, while young, should have the very best of care. The coops should be so made as to secure cleanliness, dryness, ventilation, safety, and to control the movements of the chickens. A coop of this character, which is very convenient in use, is shown in the accompanying illustrations. It is not costly, and it will pay to use it for common chickens. It is portable, having handles by which it can be lifted while closed, and moved to fresh clean ground. It therefore secures cleanliness, as ground that has been occupied by a number of chickens for a few days becomes foul and unwholesome. It is also provided with a floor-board or drawer, which can be withdrawn every day, and cleaned. If this is supplied with fresh sand or earth daily, the coop will be kept clean and sweet, and the manure

Fig. 35.

dropped may be preserved for use. It secures dryness, because it is raised from the ground by feet at the corners, and is covered with a broad sheltering roof. It has good ventilation, even when closed, by means of the wire gauze at the front, and by holes in the ends, which should also be covered with wire gauze. It is safe; no chickens can be killed in moving it; it is shut up at night, so that no rats or weasels can enter, and the chicks cannot roam abroad when the ground is wet. The movements of the hen and chickens can be controlled with facility, as the roof is hinged at the peak, and opens to admit or remove the hen. The door at the front is hinged, and, when opened, is let down to the ground, and makes a sloping platform upon which the chickens go in or out, and when closed is secured by a button. Twice in the season the coops should be whitewashed

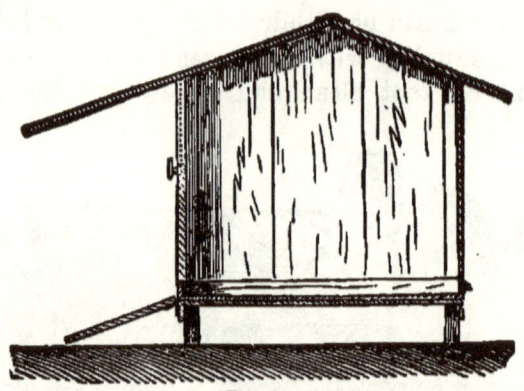

Fig. 36.

with hot fresh lime, which will keep them free from vermin. Fig. 34 shows a front view of the completed coop, arranged for two hens. Fig. 35 gives the rear view with the floor withdrawn, to be enptied and refilled, as well as the shape of the movable floor. In Fig. 36 is a sec-

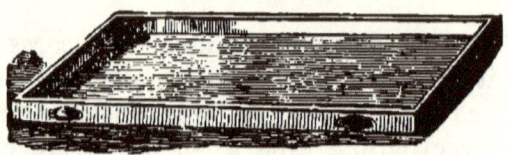

Fig. 37.

tion of the coop through the middle, showing the manner in which it is put together; and figure 37 is the drawer-floor board. There is economy in using such a coop as this, as one hen, when well cared for, may be made to bring up two or three broods together, and the hens discarded as mothers go to laying again.

CARE OF CHICKS—COOPS FOR THEM.

BOX CHICKEN-COOP.

An ordinary dry-goods box may be used for a chicken-coop. To the open end a frame or lath is fastened, thus making a run or yard for the chickens when the box is placed upon the ground, as shown in figure 38.

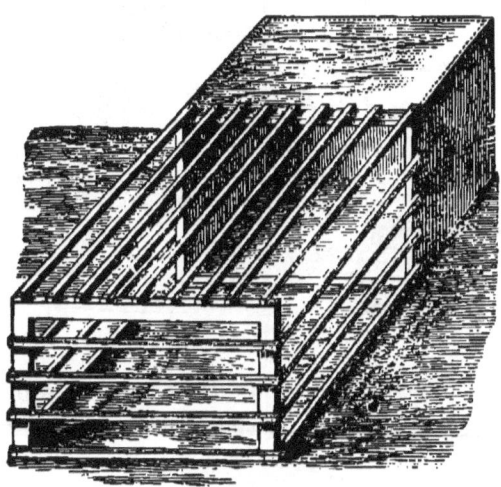

Fig. 38.

The box furnishes a comfortable place for the hen and chickens during stormy weather, an escape from the hot sun, etc. When not in use the lath frame can be taken from the box, its three sides and ends separated, and stored away for use another season.

BARREL CHICKEN-COOPS.

Any old barrel that would otherwise be thrown away may be put to good use in making a comfortable place for a hen and chickens. Brace the barrel on the two sides with bricks or stones to keep it from rolling; raise the rear enough to bring the lower edge of the open end close to the ground; drive a few stakes in front and

Fig. 39.

the coop is complete. It is best to put the barrel near a fence, that it may be all the more secure and out of

Fig. 40.

the way. Nests for turkeys may be made in the same way, in out-of-the-way places, omitting the stakes, and putting in a good supply of straw to make the nest.

CARE OF CHICKS—COOPS FOR THEM. 59

Very good chicken-coops may be made of old flour or fruit barrels. One way in which they may be made is by removing the hoops from one end, and putting them inside, in such a manner that the staves are forced apart on one side, as shown in Fig. 39. The barrel is set on the ground, with the open staves downward. On the other side of the barrel the staves should be kept close together, as a protection against the weather and vermin. Another way is to cut off the end of each alternate

Fig. 41.—FEEDING-PEN FOR CHICKS.

stave, in lines, about three inches from each other. The halves of the barrels then taken apart, and set bottom upwards, make very good coops, as shown in Fig. 40. If a piece of leather is fastened upon the top of one of these coops, so as to form a handle, it may be lifted and moved to fresh ground very readily. Young chicks, that are permitted to range with the large fowls, may be fed without interference by the others, in an inclosure which may be made as shown in Fig. 41. Common laths are sawn into proper lengths and nailed to a frame, three inches space being left for the chicks to go in and out. On one side the laths are cut off six inches from the ground, and a strip, *A*, three inches wide, is secured so as to be raised as the chicks grow larger, to permit them to pass under it. If made ten feet long and five feet wide, it will be large enough to feed 200 chicks. The frames for the sides and ends may be attached to each other by pins, or hooks and staples, and when not in use they may be taken apart and packed away until again required.

REARING EARLY CHICKENS.

Warmth is the only requisite for rearing early chickens, which one finds it difficult to provide early in the season. But there is an easy way to furnish this for the early broods, where the other conveniences are con-

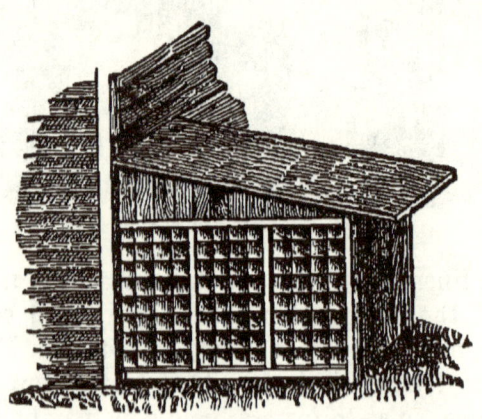

Fig. 42.

sistent with it; that is, where the poultry-house is tight and warm, and is kept clean and free from vermin, and where the fowls are fed judiciously. The illustration (Fig. 42) represents an annex to a poultry-house, made at very little cost. It was built at the end of the poultry-house, and a door from this opened into it. It measures ten by twelve feet on the ground, and seven and a half feet high at the top of the roof. It required seven common hot-bed sashes, purchased for one dollar each (three of those are shown and the other four should be seen under the overhanging eaves), and the rest of the material cost about ten dollars. The floor was the ground, which was sandy and dry, and soon became quite warm under the heat of the sun even in January. When the hens wanted to brood, they were carried in the movable nest into this warm house, where they were fed and watered daily, and could enjoy a bath in the dry, warm, sandy floor. The droppings were gathered up daily in a pail, and carried out, and the house was kept as clean and sweet as possible. When the young chicks appeared, and had been nursed in the warm brooder, which has been previously described, they were given to the hen, who was put into a coop, and usually two broods were given to each, and sometimes three. A good, quiet Light Brahma or Plymouth Rock hen will take twenty-four or twenty-five chicks and rear them all safely when thus cared for, as the warm house greatly relieves her from the work of brooding the chicks and keeping them warm. The chicks are fed four times a day, the chief food at the first being crushed wheat and coarse oatmeal, with coarse cracked corn and clean water in a shallow plate, in the center of which an inverted tin fruit-can is placed, to prevent the chicks from running through it. The advantage of such a house as this is that chicks can be reared that are fit for market so early as to bring the highest price. An instance may be given of the income from a small flock of twenty light Brahma hens for a year, from January to December, which left a clear profit of a little over seven dollars per hen. It is quite possible to do this with a flock of one hundred hens which are good brooders, kept in one house and yard, and properly kept and cared for with such help as this, to secure early broiling chickens, as these bring a high price. A brood of eight chicks, which is a fair average for each hen, sold at seventy-five cents each, will make six dollars alone, and some of the cockerels in the case mentioned sold in the fall for eighteen cents a pound, and weighed nine pounds each, making one dollar and sixty-two cents each.

BROODERS FOR EARLY CHICKENS.

The greatest profit in poultry-keeping is from the early chickens. By good feeding and management some of the hens may be brooding in January, and all the chicks may be saved by the use of artificial brooders. Incubators are used by experts with success, but farmers and ordinary poultry-keepers are rarely successful with these machines. Brooders, however, may be used by any person, even a boy or girl, who will simply see that the heat is not excessive, and when the chicks open their mouths, give them fresh air. Eighty degrees is quite enough warmth for newly hatched chicks, which are taken from the nest as they come out, and are placed in the brooder until all the brood is out, when they may be removed to a warm, glazed coop, with the hen. Young chicks have been thus nursed until they were strong, which ran about in the snow in February with great pleasure and comfort, and not one was lost out of a lot of ninety, which were all hatched in January. All that is required is to have a warm part of the buildings or an attic room for the setting hens, and glazed coops set in a sunny place out of doors for the chicks when they come from the brooder. The brooder (fig. 43) is a box eighteen inches square or thereabouts, one end opening as a door and closing tight, lined with hair felt, or blanket cloth, and having a shelf in the middle, and a glass in the upper half of the door, so that the chicks may be seen. A tin heater having handles and a screw-opening to put in the hot water, fits into the lower part, which is also lined with the felt or double blanket. The heater is filled with boiling water and put in its place, wrapped in a piece of blanket to retain the heat and moderate it. A nest, covered with a sheet of paper, which can be removed when soiled, is put on the shelf. A pasteboard box, upon half-inch cleats, makes a good nest. A thermometer is kept in the nest, so that the

Fig. 43.

warmth may be regulated by putting more blanket over the heater, or by ventilating the brooder by holes in the door, closed by corks. Chipped eggs will be hatched in such a brooder; weak chicks may be saved, and all the losses by chicks being crushed in the nest are avoided. The heat is admitted to the nest by holes in the shelf.

Another brooder is shown at Fig. 44. This is a larger and shallower box, having a tray in the upper part with a slatted or wire gauze floor, upon which the heater rests; a lid is made to cover this tray. This heat descends through the floor of the tray into the lower part of the brooder, which is hung closely with short folds of flannels or woolen cloth for the chicks to nestle among. This is shown in the illustration. A glazed cover is put over the front of the brooder where the chicks are fed. Newly hatched chicks do not want feeding for twenty-four hours or more, but they will drink some water (or, better, *milk*) eagerly, and this should be supplied to them in a shallow plate. If one is taken in the hand and its beak is dipped in the water,

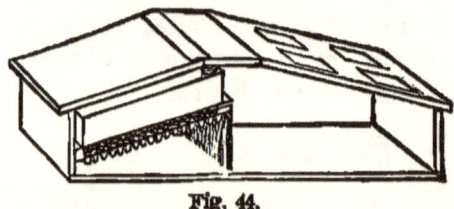

Fig. 44.

it learns to drink at once. Crumbs of corn bread or cracked wheat are good food for such young chicks while they are in the brooder. It will interest some persons to know that in some hospitals in Paris similar warm brooders have been used for weakly infants for many years, and the writer saw them there thirty years ago, used in almost precisely the same manner as is here described for the previously mentioned brooder for chicks (Fig. 43).

CHAPTER VII.

ARTIFICIAL INCUBATION.

INCUBATORS AND BROODERS.

In endeavoring to lay before our readers something that may be to their advantage, I will avail myself of the opportunity of describing that which is in *practical operation*, and do not call upon others to assist me in solving theories. There are hundreds of methods of hatching chicks artificially, as nothing more is necessary than keeping the eggs for three weeks under certain conditions of heat and moisture. What are those conditions, and why do failures occur so often, even when every attention is given the process?

In the first place, there are a great many unforeseen difficulties in the way that are overlooked or not anticipated. An incubator cannot hatch every fertile egg, neither can the hen do so; yet there are some manufacturers who claim that the incubators made by them will hatch every fertile egg. To test the hatching of fertile eggs, I procured eggs from two different places. After placing them in the same incubator, and at the same time, I removed all clear eggs by the tenth day. Of the first lot of fifty eggs thirty-two were fertile, and of the second lot of fifty there were thirty-four fertile eggs. The eggs of the first lot hatched thirty chicks, while every chick of the second lot perished in the shell. Upon investigation, I found that the fowls from which the eggs of the first lot had been procured were in full health, and had plenty of exercise, a cockerel of about one year of age being mated with two-year old hens. The eggs of the second lot were from hens that were mated with a brother, and the flock had been bred in for three years. The consequence was that while there was life in each egg there was not sufficient vitality in the chick to enable it to break out.

There are numerous reasons for not expecting full hatches. Eggs from pullets do not always hatch, nor do those from hens that are very fat; yet such eggs may be fertile. Eggs that have been chilled will sometimes contain chicks that have advanced to the stage of ten days, when placed in an incubator; besides, frequent handling, or delay in placing them in the incubator, may also affect the result. Hence, the first and most important matter is to use eggs specially secured for the purpose. The hen that steals her nest, by running at large, and having all the privileges and advantages of exercise, hatches nearly all the eggs, for the reason that if one hatches all should do so, as they have the same parentage, while we are compelled to use eggs from different hens, but few of them being alike in any respect. The hen deposits her eggs where they are seldom disturbed, while we subject them to frequent handling and changeable temperatures. It is doubtful if any farmer would consider himself unlucky if he succeeded in raising seven chicks out of every ten hatched; yet this proportion is equal to a loss of thirty in every hundred. If, therefore, an incubator be used, this should be considered, and when the loss is apparently heavy, a comparison should be made with the work done by hens, which will, as a rule, be in favor of the incubator and brooder.

Having stated what the conditions should be, so far as the eggs are concerned, the next step is to consider the defects existing in many of the incubators that are placed upon the market; and as I am not a manufacturer, nor interested in the sale of incubators, I have no object in view other than a desire to correct some of the mistakes that have been made in the construction of incubators. The supposition that a constant stream of pure air must flow through an incubator is, in my opinion, an error. Not that there should not be plenty of pure air, but it should not pass through as a current. The hen on the nest airs the eggs, but she keeps the air still and motionless. The desire to regulate an incubator has caused incubators to be constructed that open and shut off the heat very easily; but an observer may notice that they will often open and close the valves every few minutes, thus causing the heat to change in as many times, and to allow of slow or fast currents according to the degree of frequency with which the valves open and shut. The best machines are those that *slowly* reach a point above or below the normal hatching point. Too much air passes into the incubators and not enough in the brooders, as a rule. A little chick does not require so large a volume of air as is usually allowed, and a hundred of them together will not consume so much as a small quadruped. If the air is admitted below the eggs, there will always enough escape to allow fresh air to enter for ventilation. We now hatch them, in our section, in incubators holding 400 eggs each, by closing the drawer, allowing no mode of ventilation other than to keep three or four one-inch tubes open at the bottom of the incubator, and the chicks remain thus shut up for twenty-four hours at a time without inconvenience. In fact, by leaving them in the drawer they are thoroughly dry and prepared for the brooder when taken out. A regulator should be a very simple arrangement. Some of them are so delicate in construction as to do more injury than good, and it is often the case that the *regulator* instead of the incubator must be watched. The majority of persons put too much *faith* in the regulator, relying upon it too implicitly, and often fail in consequence. Other incubators regulate the heat very well, but cannot do away with the work of watching the flame of the lamps. The flame must be regulated according to the temperature of the outside atmosphere. To be successful the operator must determine that he will do the work himself, and he must *watch* the incubator, whether it regulates or not. He who attempts to raise chickens artificially by using a self-regulating incubator without expecting to do anything except to trust to the machine, will always be of the opinion that incubators are humbugs. It means work and attention every time, but it is work that pays if well bestowed.

In Hammonton we do not use any self-regulators at all. Our incubators are simply tanks surrounded by sawdust, made by placing the sawdust between an inner and larger box, the tank being in the top of the inner box. The tank for a hundred-egg incubator is 15x30 inches, 7 inches deep, and rests on strips around the edges, with half-inch rods under it every six inches to support the weight of water. The egg-drawer is 15x36 inches, 6 inches fitting in the space at the opening when the drawer is shut. This space in the front of the egg-drawer is also boxed off and filled with sawdust. The ventilator is six inches deep, the egg-drawer three inches deep inside. Two tin tubes, one inch in diameter, are placed at the bottom of the ventilator to admit air. Four inches of sawdust surround the inner box. A tube on top of the tank, which passes through the boxes, allows water to be poured in, while a spigot in front, over the egg-drawer, permits it to be drawn off. This tank is filled with *boiling water*. The eggs are hatched at 103 degrees. The heat is regulated by drawing off a bucket of water night and morning. The eggs are turned twice a day. Moisture is supplied with boxes of moist sand under the egg-drawer, and by a few wet sponges in the egg-drawer.

These incubators do not require any *watching*. No one gets up in the night to look after them. The large body of sawdust absorbs heat, and gives it up to the egg-drawer as it begins to cool; hence, the heat varies very slowly. If a lamp is preferred, it may be attached by having two tubes, one above the other, extending to a small "boiler" outside, which is heated by a lamp, capable of accurate regulation, in the usual way.

HOW TO MAKE AN INCUBATOR.

To make this incubator, get your tinner to make you a tank fifteen inches wide, thirty inches long, and twelve inches deep, of galvanized iron or zinc, the iron being preferable. On the top should be a tube one inch in diameter and eight inches high. In front should be another tube, nine inches long, to which should be attached a spigot.

Having made your tank, have what is called the ventilator made, which is a wooden box with a bottom, but no top. The ventilator should be eight inches deep, and one inch smaller all around than the tank, as the tank must rest on inch boards, placed upright to support it, or on iron rods. In the ventilator should be two or three tin tubes, one half inch in diameter and six inches long. They should extend through the bottom, so as to admit air from below, and to within two inches of the top, or a little less.

Now make an egg-drawer, which is a frame of wood, three inches deep, having no top or bottom, except at the front, where it is boxed off and filled with sawdust, which is covered over afterward with a piece of muslin, or boards, to keep the sawdust from spilling. Of course, the egg-drawer must be made longer than the tank and ventilator, in order to allow for this space which it fills in the opening, which is the packing all around the incubator. The bottom of the egg-drawer should be made by nailing a few slats lengthwise to the under side, or rather fitting them in nicely, and over the slats in the inside of the drawer a piece of thick, strong muslin should be tightly drawn. On this muslin the eggs are placed in the same position as if laid in a hen's nest. It allows the air to pass through to the eggs for ventilation.

Having prepared the tank, let it be covered with a close-fitting box, but the box must not have any bottom. This is to protect the tank against pressure of water on the sides, and to assist in retaining heat. Such being done, place your ventilator first, egg-drawer next, and tank last. Now place a support under the tank and the box, or have them rest on rods, and as the weight of water will be great in the centre, the iron rods should be placed crosswise under the tank every six inches. Now fasten the three apartments (ventilator, egg-drawer, and tank) together, with boards nailed to the sides and back and front (of course leaving the opening for the egg-drawer), care being taken to drive no nails in the egg-drawer, as it must move in and out, and should have a strong strip to rest on for that purpose. Having completed these preparations, make a larger box to go over all three, so that there will be a space on the sides, back, front, and on top, but as the ventilator must be filled with sawdust to within one inch of the top of the tubes, it serves for the bottom packing. Make the outer box so that there will be room for filling all around the inside box with sawdust, and also on top, being careful to let the tube for pouring in the water come through, as also the spigot in front. The front of the incubator must be packed also. The incubator should be raised from the floor about an inch, when completed, to allow the air to pass under and thence into the ventilator tubes.

The incubator being complete, the tank is filled with boiling water. It must remain untouched for twenty-four hours, as it requires time during which to heat completely through. As it will heat slowly, it will also cool slowly. Let it cool down to 110°, and then put in the eggs, or, what is better, run it without eggs for a day or two in order to learn it, and notice its variation. When the eggs are put in, the drawer will cool down some. All that is required then is to add about a bucket or so of hot water once or twice a day, but be careful about endeavoring to get up heat suddenly, as the heat does not rise for five hours after the additional bucket of water is added. The tank radiates the heat down on the eggs, there being nothing between the iron bottom of the tank and the eggs, for the wood over and around the tank does not extend across the *bottom* of the tank. The cool air comes from below in the ventilator pipes, passing through the muslin bottom of the egg-drawer to the eggs. The 15x30 inch tank incubator holds 100 eggs. Lay the eggs in, the same as in a nest, promiscuously.

In regard to the sawdust packing. The bottom board is wider than the ventilator. Each corner of this bottom board should be 2 x 3 well-fitted posts, the posts being six inches (or whatever height desired), higher than the three compartments (ventilator, egg-drawer, and tank) when the three are in position. To these posts fasten tongued and grooved boards, and you will then have the compartments enclosed with a larger box. Now fill in your sawdust (sides and top), covering the top sawdust with the same kinds of boards, first boring a hole for the tube on top, or fitting the boards around it by bringing two boards together on a line with the tube, each having a crescent cut into them thus ( ). Be sure and fasten up the compartments by nailing them together in such a manner that no sawdust can get in the egg-drawer, and be careful to drive no nails into the egg-drawer when fastening the three compartments. As the tank should be covered with wood, it is best to fasten

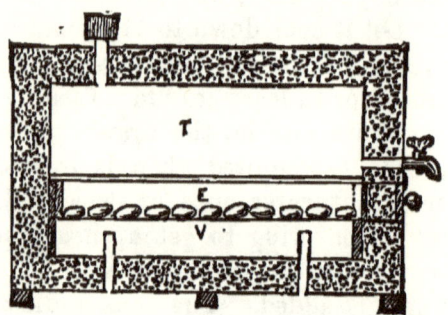

Fig. 45.—SECTION OF INCUBATOR.

the three parts together before making the *outer* box which holds the sawdust, by nailing upright strips closely together, fastening the top end to the wood surrounding the tank, and the bottom ends to the sides of the ventilator. We show in Fig. 45 a sectional view of the incubator.

DIRECTIONS.

To give the directions plainly, in order to avoid compelling our readers to write us, we will repeat them, and be as precise as possible:

The incubator should be filled with *boiling* water. It will take a large quantity, but once filled it will remain so. Let it remain shut up for twenty-four hours, in order to allow the heat to go all through it. Always look at the thermometer *as quickly as possible*, as it varies quickly. The drawer should be at 103 degrees, and if warmer than that leave the drawer out a little while until it cools down, always shutting it up first, in order to let the heat accumulate a moment or two before looking at the thermometer. Never try to cool it with cold water, for the heat is in the packing, and you can never tell what the effect will be for several hours. Should you add hot water, it will be from two to four hours before the increased heat appears. It is due to this fact that the incubator is so reliable, as the heating and cooling is gradual. When the thermometer reaches 110° put in the eggs. The eggs will cool the drawer, but do not be alarmed. Let them remain for an hour or two, and if the temperature is then below 100°, add a kettleful of water (nearly a bucketful), which will return the heat to about 103° in an hour or two. If the weather is moderate, once a day will only be necessary for adding water, but the better way to work the incubator is to divide the twenty-four hours into three periods of eight hours each, say 6 o'clock A.M., 2 P.M., and 10 P.M., when a gallon of water may be added at each time, and the eggs turned. This avoids late night work, and gives but little trouble.

Be sure and practice with the incubator for three or four days before putting in the eggs, for by so doing you will know just how much water to use.

The colder the weather the more hot water. All incubators do best in an even temperature.

Keep a pan of water in the ventilator, changing it to fresh water daily.

Keep the heat as near 103° as possible, and the last three days not over 102°.

Take the drawer out in the morning and let it remain out for the eggs to cool down to 70°. Then turn the eggs half way round, and place the drawer back. Make a mark on each side of the egg in order to be guided in knowing which side is up correctly. Turn them morning and night, but cool them down only once a day.

Always keep a few wet sponges in the egg-drawer, as they will indicate the moisture. Put the thermometer in among the centre of the eggs, the top of the bulb on a line with the top of the eggs, the upper end of the thermometer kept slightly raised.

Three weeks are required for hatching, and the temperature should not get below 98° nor over 105°. Should the eggs be over-heated, let them cool well, sprinkle them, and put them back. Heat as high as 108° for a *short time* is not necessarily fatal. Never sprinkle as long as the sponge keeps moist, and always sprinkle with tepid water.

. *BE SURE your thermometer is correct,* as one half of them are incorrect, the low-priced ones being as true as the highest-priced ones. Place your thermometer next to a hen's body under the wing; shut down the wing closely upon it; let it remain so for a minute. Then quickly look at the thermometer, and it should be at 104°. It is best, however, to have it tested in a pan of warm water, by the side of one known to be correct.

Do not keep the incubator where there are any odors.

When the chicks hatch do not remove them until they are dry; then put them in the brooder. Keep the heat in the brooder at not less than 90°. Feed at first hard-boiled eggs for a day or two. No food should be given the first twenty-four hours. Then feed oat-meal and corn-meal, cooked and moistened with milk. Feed four or five times a day, at first, for a week. Keep fine screenings, cracked corn, fine gravel, fine-ground oyster-shells, pulverized charcoal, and clean water always where they can get at such, and keep everything *clean.* Give mashed potatoes, chopped onions, or cabbage, or anything that serves as a *variety.* Be sure and not *crowd* them. Divide them into small lots. Feed in little troughs.

An egg-drawer two feet wide and three feet long will hold one hundred and fifty eggs with an egg-turner. A drawer three feet wide and four feet long holds three hundred eggs. Only one drawer can be used to an incubator.

BROODERS.

The principal conditions necessary in a brooder are plenty of *fresh* air and sufficient heat to prevent the chicks from crowding. We have a building here, now in operation, divided into ten apartments, each apartment being five by seven feet and accommodating one hundred chicks. The building is fifty feet long and ten feet wide, and a passage way running its whole length, and taking up three feet of the ten, leaving the spaces for the chicks seven feet. The yards are sixteen feet long and five feet wide. The chicks are all brooded with a stove. To describe how it is done, we will explain that Fig. 46 is a box six inches deep, three feet wide, and fifty feet long. Two-inch iron pipes are arranged as shown in the illustration, the top of the box being removed to show the interior. The hot water may be supplied by an ordinary stove " water back," or by a coil of pipe in a stove. This is heated by a piece of pipe one inch in diameter, coiled in a stove, holes being cut in the stove for the purpose of admitting pipes. The hot water flows out and the cold water flows in. The floor of the box is made close, with tongued and grooved boards. The cold air enters through tubes reaching to the outside of the building. It is heated by coming in contact with the pipes, and enters into the tubes on the top of the floor, which are two and a half inches high. Over these tubes are little tables, one yard square and three inches high, with strips of cloth tacked around the edges.

The advantages of this brooder are, that it gives the heat from the top, as the warm air strikes the under side of the table (or brooder) and diffuses itself over the chicks, which cannot crowd easily, as there are no sides or corners. The warm air is pure, as it comes in fresh from the outside, and serves as heat and ventilation at the same time. Figs. 46 and 47 show the *ground* plan. The building has a window to each apartment, which is hung to a weight, so as to move up or down. Hence, when the window is up each apartment becomes a shed, open to the south. The chicks have a sand floor to scratch in, and are allowed to run in the yards when two weeks old.

This building, together with the heating arrangements, did not cost over one hundred dollars. The chicks are about ready for market, and are expected to realize six hundred dollars gross. The cost for feeding the chicks to the age of ten weeks is ten cents. The total cost, including the value of eggs, food, and other expenses is about nine cents per pound. They will average one and a half pounds when eight weeks old, and often bring fifty cents per pound. The building contains one thousand chicks, and as a new brood can be put in every ten weeks, it will hold five thousand in a year. The building and yards do not take up more than twenty-six by fifty feet of space, or less than one thirtieth of an acre.

The chicks are fed on hard-boiled eggs the second day, no food being given them the first day. Then milk and bread are allowed. On the fourth day they are fed on a mixture of one part corn meal, one part bran, and one part middlings, with a small quantity of bone meal and ground or finely chopped meat. They are fed five times a day till feathered, then four meals are

ARTIFICIAL INCUBATION. 77

given. Chopped cabbage, onions, and other green food are supplied. Skimmed milk may be used in the food, which should always be scalded or cooked. Plenty of water, gravel and dry earth are kept before them, a few screenings being scattered in the dirt to induce them to scratch. In giving water never allow them to become

Fig. 46.—INTERIOR OF BROODER BOX.
Showing hot-water pipes and cold-air pipes.

wet, as dampness is fatal. Avoid *bottom* heat in a brooder, as it causes leg weakness. It is always better to have too much heat in the brooder than too little, but the reverse is the case with an incubator.

A light, sandy soil is best for chicks. Hence, poor

Fig. 47.—TOP OF BROODER BOX.
Showing one of the brooder tables, and one space with table removed to show hot-air tube.

and unproductive locations can be thus used with advantage. Chicks require unceasing care, but by raising them in large numbers, labor may be economized. They need no care at night, other than to keep up the fire, which may be arranged so as to give sufficient heat till morning. They should be fed very *early* and *late*.

When ready for market correspond with a reliable commission merchant before shipping.

We have two or three large broiler establishments here. In one case two young ladies are hatching several thousand chicks annually, and they find it very profitable.

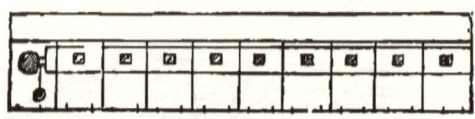

Fig. 48.—GROUND PLAN OF BUILDING.

Showing brooders, stove, and water-barrel.

As stated, nearly all the failures come from the *eggs*, and not the incubators, and until poultrymen realize this fact they will meet with disappointment. The loss does not exceed seven per cent, and that includes the weak chicks and all that die by accident. No gapes or lice effect them, as everything is kept very clean. As to what may

Fig. 49.—STOVE, WATER BARREL, AND END OF BROODER BOX.

be expected it may be stated that if fifty chicks are marketed from every one hundred eggs used, the result will be satisfactory, but this includes loss of bad eggs, dead chicks, and other causes. The chicks grow faster than when with hens, as they receive better care and can be

ARTIFICIAL INCUBATION. 79

counted at any time. They are safe from all enemies. My advice to beginners is to begin with a small incubator, and experiment the first year. Experience will be the best teacher. Do not expect too much, and do not expect to

Fig. 50.—BROODER HOUSE, WITH YARDS OMITTED.

raise chicks without work. Watching, care, and labor are essentials. No incubator or brooder, however well regulated, can be trusted. They are treacherous. But they will return a handsome profit if properly managed.

CHAPTER VIII.

PREPARING FOR MARKET.

FATTENING POULTRY.

No fowl over two years old should be kept in the poultry-yard except for some special reason. An extra good mother or a finely feathered bird that is desirable as a breeder may be preserved until ten years old with advantage, or at least so long as she is serviceable. But ordinary hens and cocks should be fattened at the end of the second year for market. When there is a room or shed that can be closed, the fowls may be confined there. The floor should be covered with two or three inches of fine sawdust, dry earth, sifted coal-ashes, or clean sand. The food should be given four times a day, and clean water be always before the fowls. A dozen or more fowls may be put at once in each apartment. One of the best foods for rapid fattening, for producing well-flavored flesh and rich fat, is buckwheat meal, mixed with sweet skimmed milk, into a thick mush. A teaspoonful of salt should be stirred in the food for a dozen fowls. Two weeks' feeding is sufficient to fatten the fowls, when they should be shipped for sale without delay and other lots put up for feeding. If the fattening-coop is kept dark and cool, as it should be, the fowls will fatten all the quicker for it.

WHEN TO MARKET.

Poultry which it is not intended to winter should be fattened before really severe weather comes on; otherwise money will be lost by them. They will barely hold their own in December on feed which caused them to increase rapidly in weight a month earlier. Those who have watched the market know that autumn prices usually are highest a little before and a little after Thanksgiving, say about the middle of November and soon after the first of December. The reason is that those who are fattening fowls keep them back for a short time before Thanksgiving-day and before Christmas-time, in order to get them in prime order for sale at those times. The result is usually an over-stocked market and plenty of cheap poultry. Soon after the first of January prices go up again; and well they may, for one or two months' feed has been consumed and very little weight added.

Capons grow rapidly, and their growth takes up the food, so that we have to wait until growth stops before they fatten. It is well, therefore, that this delicious class of poultry should not make its appearance before the first of February, when the game-laws prohibit venison, quail, and other choice game from being exposed for sale. At this time, consequently, fat capons and pullets meet a good market, and even during Lent, when a considerable portion of the Christian world abstain from meats, there is a sharp demand for the highest-prized meats to grace the table of the rich on Sundays. It is therefore well to have fine capons ready to supply this demand.

DRESSING AND SHIPPING.

The directions sent to their customers by Messrs. E. & O. Ward, 279 Washington Street, one of the oldest commission houses in New York City, though very brief and concise, give the results of an extensive experience and present all the essential points in dressing and shipping for that market. They say: "To insure highest market prices for poultry, they must be well fattened; crops empty when killed; nicely and well picked and skin not broken or torn; thoroughly cooled, but not frozen. Pack in boxes with a layer of clean straw (rye-straw the best) between the layers of poultry, in the same posture in which they roost. Mark each box, specifying what it contains. Send invoice by mail. Ship to reach us about the middle of the week—should never reach us so late in the week as on Saturday.

"There is the greatest demand for fine and fat turkeys for Thanksgiving; for prime and nice geese for Christmas; for extra large and nice turkeys for New-Year's-day. On all these occasions shipments should reach us two to five days in advance. If you cannot find any profit in sending poultry of *prime* quality and well prepared, you need not look for any in that of ordinary or poor qualities."

An ordinance adopted by the Board of Aldermen of New York City, and approved by the Mayor, is as follows:

"SECTION 1. That no turkeys or chickens be offered for sale in the city unless the crops of such turkeys and chickens are free from food or other substance and shrunken close to their bodies. That all fowls exposed for sale in violation of this ordinance shall be seized and condemned; such of them as shall be tainted shall, upon examination, be destroyed, and the rest which are fit for food shall be used in the public institutions in the city.

"SECTION 2. Every person exposing for sale any chicken or turkey in contravention of this ordinance shall be liable to a penalty of five dollars for each chicken or turkey so exposed for sale."

This ordinance took effect the first day of October, 1882.

DRESSING POULTRY—THE NEW ENGLAND METHOD.

While poultry for some markets is rarely, if ever, drawn, that for the Boston and other New England markets—at least that of the better class—always has the entrails drawn when the birds are killed. There is something in favor of both methods. In the former, no air being admitted into the cavity of the body, it keeps in good condition much longer than it would if opened. On the other hand, if the poultry is kept too long there is danger that any food which may be in the crop, etc., may ferment, even if nothing worse takes place, and impregnate the flesh unpleasantly. A poultry-raiser of Ayer, Mass., gives the following directions:

"First catch the chickens. Slide your hands carefully among their legs until you can grasp the desired one; hold quite still until the neck is grasped. Cut the throat near the under side of the bill quite deeply; then with the right hand upon the legs hold the wings over the back to avoid fluttering. Always drain the blood into the chicken's pail. If the fowl is wanted for immediate use, scald it for about half a minute, being careful to get the tail and wings under. Take out and strip the legs quickly from the feet towards the head. Hold a handful of feathers in the hand, pushing the feathers from tail to head. Scald three minutes in three quarts of water. Make a small slit behind and on the side of the crop, one chick after the other. Then take out entrails and crop and windpipe, carefully removing the liver from the gall. Take the gizzard to the pail and open and skin with another knife. Cut off the head and legs, putting these in a pile. When cold, cut them up and put them into the pail for your hens. This refuse thus disposed of is worth at least one cent per fowl. By scalding one can dress about six in an hour, while dry picking is much slower."

SAVE THE FEATHERS—FEATHER-BONE.

Few persons are aware that the coarse wing-feathers of turkeys and ducks, which cannot be used for dusters, and are generally a nuisance about the farm-yard, are of any value. Large poultry-raisers especially will be glad to learn that a recent invention of Mr. E. K. Warren of Michigan has created a demand for these hitherto worthless feathers, and that a company is now manufacturing, out of the quills of feathers, an excellent substitute for whalebone, which, by the way, is becoming scarce and dear.

The feathers are first stripped of their plumage by revolving shears, then the quill is divided into halves by delicate machinery, after which the pith is removed to be used as a fertilizer. Analysis has shown it to be rich in nitrogen, and therefore very valuable on the farm. The split quills are cut into narrow shreds and braided into strong strands by machinery. These strands are in turn combined until there is produced a firm elastic band so strong that great power would be required to break it. This is sewed lengthwise many times through with colored threads, the feather-bone taking various colors from the kind of thread used. Though the business is only a few months old, a hundred persons are employed, and it is daily increasing. Patents have been secured in the leading European

PREPARING FOR MARKET.

countries, and large offers have been made for the right to use feather-bone in making whips, corsets, etc., but the inventor chooses to reserve his rights. One who has never given any attention to the subject scarcely comprehends the demand for a substitute for whalebone. This commodity is said to be even better for many purposes than the whalebone which it imitates.

CHAPTER IX.

PRESERVING EGGS FOR MARKET.

To preserve eggs for a considerable time the pores of the shell must be stopped up, for two reasons : to prevent the entrance of the air, and consequent spoiling of the contents, and to prevent the evaporation of the moisture of the egg and a drying-up of the contents. There are two principal methods of doing this. One is, to smear the surface of the eggs with something that will close the pores, and then pack them in some material that will practically exclude the air. The eggs are smeared with lard, coated with linseed or cotton-seed oil, or with shellac varnish, and are afterwards packed in bran, dry sand, or other similar material. These methods will answer for home use; but whatever may be the coating material, the surface of the shells will have an unnatural appearance, which will prevent their ready sale in the markets. The only practical method to preserve eggs to be sold is to place them in milk of lime, which is another name for whitewash, and is prepared precisely as for whitewashing. The fresh eggs are packed in a barrel, and the lime-wash, well stirred and then strained, is poured over them. The eggs must be fresh when packed, and must be kept in a cool place. The eggs, according to the extent of the operations, are placed in barrels or in brick vats or tanks, built for the purpose. The dealers who handle large quantities of eggs have brick tanks built in a cool cellar. Any vessel, such as a but or barrel, will answer the purpose in a small way as well as the tanks. The eggs when sent to market are removed from the lime and thoroughly washed, and when dry are packed in barrels of cut straw, like other eggs. In the New York market they usually bring about five cents a dozen less than fresh eggs. When packing eggs for private use, it is well to wait until September, when the fowls, having had a good run on the stubble fields and about grain barns, begin to lay plentifully, and eggs become cheap. Take perfectly fresh eggs, and pack them in a butter firkin, or barrel, and pour over them milk of lime, or thick lime-wash, after it has cooled, and head up the keg; or pour over them the strongest brine; or smear the eggs with cottonseed or linseed oil, and pack them on their broad ends in wheat bran in a keg, barrel, or box, very tightly, and each week turn it over so as to reverse the position of the eggs. The last method has been found to be exceedingly satisfactory. Eggs packed in dry salt will not keep for any great length of time.

PACKING EGGS IN A BARREL.

A great number of eggs are lost every year through imperfect packing. The salable value of a package of eggs is measured by that of the poorest part of it; the good always have their value diminished by the bad; but the poor eggs are never raised in value by the good. If by poor packing any part is damaged, the whole is depreciated together. A badly packed barrel of eggs is a miserable thing to look at, and worse still to handle, especially when the weather is warm and a *very* few old nest eggs have been packed with the good ones, which does sometimes happen in spite of care, though not when only glass nest eggs, which never spoil, are used. The barrel should be a good one, clean, strong, and well hooped. At the bottom is placed three inches in depth of clean, dry, sweet rye or wheat straw, cut in a fodder-cutter into chaff not over half an inch in length. Upon this the first layer of eggs is placed on their sides, near together, but not touching. Some of the cut chaff is then scattered over the eggs, so that it falls between them and fills the spaces. Then one inch in depth of chaff is laid upon them, and another layer of eggs placed upon it. The number of eggs in each layer is marked upon a tally. An ordinary-sized flour-barrel will hold 70 dozen. It is not well to crowd more than this into a barrel. The chaff and eggs are placed in alternate layers in this way until the barrel is one-third full, when a piece of board is laid upon the chaff and pressed down carefully to make the mass solid. This is done again when the barrel is two-thirds full, and it is then shaken gently to settle the contents. When the last layer is packed, it is covered with three inches of chaff, which should project an inch or more above the chine of the barrel. When the head is pressed down steadily and slowly into its place with some shaking of the barrel, the eggs will be held so firmly that no shaking they may receive in the course of their journey will loosen them, and a severe jar will not break any of them. When they arrive at their destination they will be in good order, and bring the highest price, having cost no more to pack, except a little extra trouble, than the poorest barrel that may come to market. Musty or damp straw, or poor grain, will give a scent and flavor to the eggs which will injure them, notwithstanding it is generally supposed that an egg-shell is impervious to such influence. Cut wheat or oat straw is the best packing, wheat or oat chaff is the next; good sound oats are a good but expensive packing; hay is very poor material, and buckwheat bran the worst, as it so readily heats. When the barrel is packed, the number of eggs in it should be plainly marked upon the head.

PACKING EGGS FOR WINTER.

Of the various methods practised for preserving eggs for winter use, one of the most effective is that employed by the dealers who buy when the supply is large and prices low. This is as follows: Brick vats,

Fig. 51.—VAT FOR PICKLING EGGS.

or wooden tanks, are constructed in cool dry cellars, partly sunk below the level of the floor, as in Figure 51, the dotted lines showing the portion below the ground. These vats and tanks,—or casks, which may be used instead,—are partly filled with a preservative mixture of

Fig. 52.—EGG LADLE.

thick lime-water, or milk of lime, to which are sometimes added salt and a small quantity of cream of tartar (bi-tartrate of potash), and the eggs are placed in this mixture and kept covered. The eggs are placed in the tank by means of a peculiar dipper (Fig. 52), made of a round, shallow tin pan, with a long handle, the tin being perforated to drain off the liquid. The eggs are lowered to near the bottom, and gently rolled out, with little risk of breakage. Here they remain until required for sale. If they were fresh when packed away, they will come out after three or four months so little changed that few persons would be able to distinguish them from fresh ones. When wanted for sale they are taken out of the pickle with the dipper, and carefully placed in the crate, shown at Fig. 53. This is made of laths; but an open splint basket would answer the purpose as well.

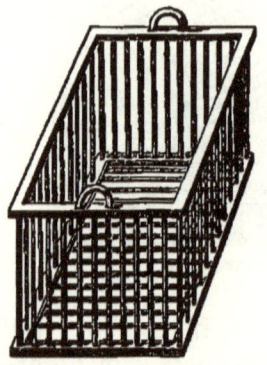 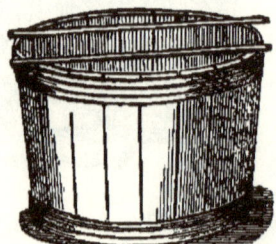

Fig. 53.—CRATE FOR IMMERS-　　Fig. 54.—TUB FOR DRAINING
　　ING EGGS.　　　　　　　　　　　THE EGGS.

A large low tub, as half a hogshead, is provided, and two boards are placed across the top, as seen in Fig. 54. The crate of eggs is placed upon the boards, and water is run through it until all perceptible traces of lime are removed. In this method of preservation there is nothing that may not be done in a small way, and with any substituted apparatus which will answer the purpose. One thing is imperative—the eggs *must* be fresh when packed, or they cannot be kept in a good condition for several months.

EGGS IN GREAT BRITAIN AND THE UNITED STATES.

The population of Great Britain was, in 1881, thirty-five millions. That of the United States, in 1880, was fifty millions. There were in Great Britain, in 1885, fowls (all kinds), 29,940,000; in the United States, in 1880, 125,507,000. Great Britain has a little over 20,000,000 of the ordinary barn-yard fowl. The remainder are ducks, geese, and turkeys. In our census, 102,000,000 are of the barn-yard kinds. The egg-product of this country is put at 457,000,000 dozen, or forty-five eggs for each fowl; that of Great Britain, at the same rate, would be 75,000,000 dozen. In 1883 Great Britain imported 71,000,000 dozen eggs, which, at the same rate for 1885, would give an aggregate of 166,000,000 dozen for home production and import, or about four dozen a head for the population. In the last year for which we have official returns, the import of eggs to the United States was 16,487,204 dozen, and our export was 295,000 dozen. The consumption of eggs in the United States, adding home production to the import, is about nine dozen for the entire population. It is no wonder the country grows so fast and vigorous, when it has at hand such stores of nutritious food.

The value of our egg import is nearly $3,000,000, as stated in the Customs returns, or about six cents a dozen. Happy is the consumer who can buy them for twelve cents. Of the egg import into the United States, three fourths comes from Canada, mostly from Quebec and Ontario. One fifth comes in by way of Vermont, and another fifth at Buffalo, another at Niagara, and another at Boston and Ogdensburg. Nearly one half of the importation is into New England, and the remainder arrives at New York, and at Niagara and Buffalo. It is a curious fact that China sends us 220,000 dozen eggs, worth $11,466, and that San Francisco reports an import of eggs to that amount exactly. John Chinaman clings closely to his native land, and to such delicacies as those eggs must be after traveling a fourth of the circuit of the globe. Our census returns show that the egg-product—the average to the laying fowl—depends much upon the accessibility to good markets, and to the exercise of care and the administration of good food. Thus, the New England States average about eighty eggs to the fowl. New York, Pennsylvania, Illinois, and Ohio average sixty, and in some of the Southern States the average is as low as forty. In some of the States, poultry is raised more for the table than for the egg-product.

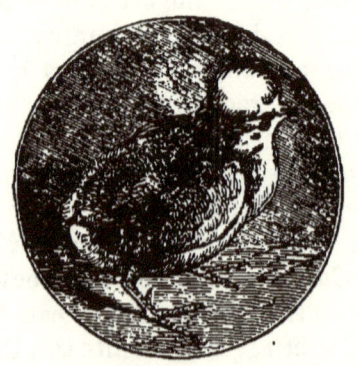

CHAPTER X.

CAPONIZING—HOW IT IS DONE.

Strange as it may seem, we have met with a number of ordinarily intelligent persons who supposed a capon to belong to a distinct race of fowls, as do Games, Bantams, etc. For fear that others may have a similar notion, it may be well to say that a capon is a castrated fowl. It bears the same relation to other male fowls that an ox does to a bull, and may be produced from any breed of fowls. A capon brings in market 50 per cent more than an ordinary fowl, and often double the price of a common male bird; besides, a capon will reach double the weight of a common fowl at the same age. As there is no difficulty whatever in caponizing, and the instruments cost very little, the practice might become very general.

Capon raising is a profitable branch of poultry culture which is not likely to be over done. The art of caponizing is easily learned. A neighbor of the writer learned to practice it a few years ago, and last year raised a large number of these delicious fowls. He informed me that he lost not more than two per cent, and that there is no need of losing any if the birds are empty of food, and the operator has sufficient light to do his work well. Good fat capons will bring fifty per cent more per pound than other fowls will sell for, and very large capons much more than that. The conditions for success are the possession of hens of a large breed, and the use of judicious crosses to produce quick growth with hardiness of constitution and aptitude to lay on flesh.

A poultry producer of large experience says: "Having practiced the operation for several years, the writer

94   PROFITS IN POULTRY.

can truly say that by using no more care, and with
no more skill, than is needed in operating upon a
male pig, not more than one out of 30 or 40 fowls need
be lost. For several years the writer has operated on
from 12 to 30 fowls each year, and the loss during that
time has not been more than five or six birds in all.
The operation is best performed upon chickens about 3
months old, although it will succeed, if carefully done,

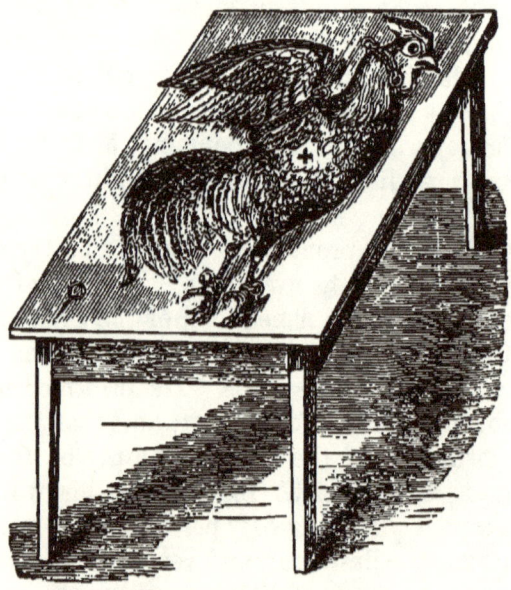

Fig. 55.—CAPONIZING TABLE.

with the majority of fowls when they are 10 or 12 months
old. As with many other operations, this is one that
can be learned most readily by seeing it done, and we
advise those who would undertake it to procure instruc-
tion wherever it is available. Still, if one has a little
confidence, he will meet with success if the directions
here given are carefully followed. In the first place, a
table is needed in which a few screw-eyes are inserted

CAPONIZING—HOW IT IS DONE. 95

at convenient places; these are furnished with broad tapes, by which the bird is securely held during the operation. The best plan for a novice is to kill a bird and operate upon that first, in order to learn the position of the parts. Lay the dead bird upon the table, dispose it as hereafter described, and then place the screw-eyes where they would be needed to secure a live fowl.

"One or two will be required to hold the wings, and one for each leg; six will be all that will ever be necessary. Place the bird upon the table and fasten it down upon its left side, as shown at Fig. 55, where the rings and tapes are seen. The spot where the opening is to be made is shown by the x. Here the feathers are plucked,

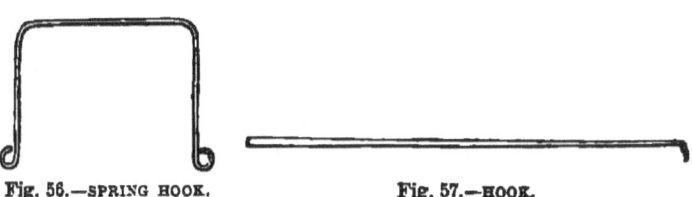

Fig. 56.—SPRING HOOK.   Fig. 57.—HOOK.

and an opening is made through the skin with a pair of shart-pointed, long-bladed scissors. We have found these better than a knife. The skin is drawn to one side and an opening is made with the scissors between the last two ribs for an inch and a half in length, great care being taken not to wound the intestines. The ribs are then separated by the spring hook (Fig. 56), so as to expose the inside. The intestines are gently moved out of the way with the handle of a teaspoon, and the glands or testicles will be seen attached to the back. The tissue which covers them is torn open with the hook (Fig. 57) aided by the tweezers (Fig. 58).

"The gland is then grasped with the forceps (Fig. 59) and the cord is held by the tweezers. The gland is then twisted off by turning the forceps; and when this has been done, the other one is removed in the same way. Care must be taken not to injure the blood-vessel which is connected with the organs, as this is the only seat of danger in the operation, and its rupture will generally be fatal. The hook is then removed, and if the skin has been drawn backward at the outset it will now slip

Fig 58.—TWEEZERS.

forward and cover the inner skin which covers the intestines, and close the opening. No stitching is needed. A few feathers are drawn together on each side of the opening and plastered down upon the skin with the blood, where they will dry and form the best possible covering to the wound, which will begin to heal at once. The bird should be fed with a very little soft bread and milk for a few days after the operation, but should have

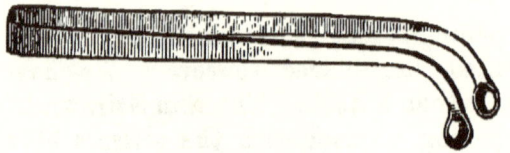

Fig. 59.—FORCEPS.

plenty of water. For two nights and one day before the operation no food nor water should be given to the birds; this will greatly facilitate the work and reduce the chances of loss. The operation, after a few successful trials, may be performed in less than one minute, and by the use of the rings and tapes, no assistance is needed. Capons may be made to earn their food by fostering young chicks, to which business they take very kindly.

CAPONIZING—HOW IT IS DONE.

To bring them to their full and most profitable size, they should be kept until the second year. By giving them corn-meal steeped in warm milk, and providing a warm house, they will grow during the whole winter, and their flesh will become very white, sweet, and juicy. A good capon of one of the large breeds will weigh 12 to 15 pounds at 22 months old, and will bring at the holiday season $2.50 to $3 each."

CHAPTER XI.

POULTRY-KEEPING AS A BUSINESS.

One newspaper correspondent asks how many fowls will support a family of six persons, as though it was a matter of figures, and only necessary to procure a certain number of fowls and a house, and start them laying eggs and producing chickens to secure a permanent income. Now it is quite safe to say that any person who knows so little about the trouble and risks of poultry-keeping as this would fail in it and lose his money, unless he should start with a dozen or two fowls, and go through an apprenticeship to the business. For a certain class of persons poultry-keeping is a very appropriate business, and may be made profitable. Those who are possessed of plenty of patience and perseverance, kindness and gentleness of disposition, a scrupulous love of order and cleanliness, a habit of close observation and quick perception, and a ready tact in finding out the cause when anything goes wrong, and in quickly remedying it, will generally succeed in keeping poultry, while those not so endowed will generally fail, and should never attempt it. Again, one must be able to justly appreciate either the difficulties or advantages of his location, such as the character of the land and its surroundings, the supply of food and the available markets. It would be folly to keep fowls on the borders of a forest or the margin of a swamp, on account of the vermin which such places shelter; it would be a great advantage to be located near a number of summer boarding-houses, where there is a good demand for eggs and chickens, or near a large city, where early plump chickens sell sometimes for 75 cents a pound, and where cheap food in the shape of various kinds of offal can be procured. A want of knowledge how to seize upon all the advantages that may offer, or to avoid the difficulties presented, will be fatal to success. Upon the character of the ground will depend greatly the kind of buildings needed. Buildings suitable for flocks of poultry kept for business and profit, where the available ground is of small extent, are shown in other chapters. The crops must be raised for food or shelter for the chickens, and to encourage the presence of insects, upon which the young chicks may feed. Sheltered by the rows of corn-stalks, or the stalks of rye or potatoes, the chicks are safe from hawks, which will not swoop down upon them except in clear ground. The coops are kept in or near this plot, being moved daily to fresh ground. The chickens are kept busy scratching in the loose ground, and there are few potatoes raised but what are scratched out and eaten by them. This furnishes them with employment and with some wholesome food, and it is for this purpose alone they are planted. If the owner of such a chicken farm is a gardener or florist, and his wife manages the poultry part of the business, producing every year two or three hundred pairs of chickens for market, besides eggs and old fowls, success may be deemed reasonably certain.

MONEY MADE BY POULTRY KEEPING.

It seems that the interest in poultry is increasing, and that more poultry keepers, instead of being absorbed by the insane idea that every one is going to get rich by selling fancy eggs at $3 a dozen, or poultry ready to lay at $3 to $5 a piece, are giving attention to raising eggs in winter, broilers in spring and summer, fat pullets in autumn, and capons in winter. In these products there is steady and sure profit. Of course a few will succeed as breeders of fancy fowls, but the number is limited, and they must have good judgment and perceptions, with persistence and perseverance.

ADVANTAGE OF CROSS BREEDING.

What breeds to cross is a problem which has not yet been solved. Asiatic fowls were bred pure, and also mated with Plymouth Rocks, which itself is a recognized cross-breed, but an established one. The result was that the cross-breed pullets and cockerels are several pounds heavier than the Asiatic pure-bred ones, which have had equally good care, feed, and other conditions of growth. Those cross-bred chickens, instead of making a great growth of *stilts* at first, and subsequently laying a modicum of flesh and fat upon them, are always ready for the table, and profitable to send to market, after they are as large as quails. The first cross makes, as a rule, the greatest improvement upon the parent breeds, and a number of practical questions come up, in regard to the subject of poultry raising, with the view simply to produce the largest amount of meat which will bring the highest price in the market. For instance, as in the crossing of Brahmas and Plymouth Rocks, or any Asiatics, with games, should the hens be of the larger breed, or the reverse? Which breeds crossed will develop the greatest early maturity? The greatest weight at the most profitable ages? The greatest weight and plumpness at the best market periods? Which makes the best capons? There have been a good many half-made efforts to solve these and kindred problems, but it can hardly be said that definite conclusions have been arrived at.

CHAPTER XII.

HINTS ABOUT MANAGEMENT.

COMMON SENSE IN THE POULTRY-YARD.

The "poultry" that everybody keeps are technically designated "Fowls," or "Barn-door Fowls." As a rule they are kept in small flocks, fed chiefly upon what no farmer misses. On most farms a flock of twelve to forty hens will pick up a living without receiving a particle of grain from May to October, including both months. Their food consists of insects, seeds, and grass or weeds; they need fresh water besides. What wonder is it that fowls thus kept are demonstrably more profitable than any class of stock, or any crop on the farm?

This is the best way to keep fowls, provided they can be induced to lay where their eggs can be found while fresh. To accomplish this a house of some kind is needed where the fowls may be shut in occasionally for a few days at a time, so as to make them roost and lay in convenient places. If fowls can roost in the trees, lay all over the farm, and "dust" themselves in the road, they will almost surely be healthy, lay a great many eggs, and keep in good condition. Besides, every now and then a hen will unexpectedly appear with a brood of ten or a dozen chicks, hatched under some bush where she had "stolen" her nest and done her hatching. That is all very well, so far as the hen is concerned, but no one wants it to happen. We wish the hens to lay and sit where we can put what eggs we please under them for hatching—and, what is still more important, we wish to be able to collect the eggs for use or for sale daily. A *fresh* egg is a joy, a delight, a good gift of Heaven—a *pretty good* egg is an abomination. An egg, to be fit to eat, or for sale, must be fresh beyond a peradventure, and utterly untainted with a suspicion of having been brooded or weathered. For this reason it is a most untidy thing to use natural nest-eggs. The nest-egg, after a while, is almost surely gathered, and of course is not "right."

The trouble about fowl-houses, even with liberal yards, is that fowls do not do well constantly confined. The number of eggs falls off, and the fowls become subject to disease, and especially to vermin—lice. All poultry-houses are liable to become thus infested, and the only cure and preventive is dust, and dustiness. It is best to provide extensive dusting-boxes—not out-of-doors somewhere, or under a cow-shed, where the fresh winds will carry off the stifling dust rendered disgusting by its "henny" smell; but in the house itself, so that the atmosphere of the entire establishment will become thus dust-laden and oppressive. Dust will settle everywhere, and one entering will need a white coat as much as does a miller. The hens will revel in the dust, however, and it will keep the lice down if not exterminate them.

The hens not only enjoy it, but dust is a necessity and a luxury to them, just as a morning bath is to civilized man. The dusting-box is their toilet-table—in fact, bath-tub, wash-bowl and pitcher, sponge and brushes and soap, and it gives health and long life as surely as the free use of water does to human beings.

As to feed—if fowls are confined they lose a great variety of food which must be, in some way, made up to them. When we depart from a close following after nature, we begin to complicate matters. Watch a hen as she trips picking about: now she takes a bit of grass or other greens; now she strips the seeds out of the seed-pod of some weed; now she makes a vigorous dive after an insect, and so on all day she scratches and forages. So a variety is essential to the health of fowls in confinement. They need grain and soft food, chopped scraps, or other flesh diet, and some grass, or other greens which they like—such as lettuce or cabbages. They must have plastering, oyster-shells pounded fine, or some other source of lime, besides fresh water constantly.

Better than all, they need an afternoon run, and a chance to scratch and pick in the door-yard, road, and barn-yard, if there be one. Here let us protest against hens being made use of as scavengers for picking up and cleaning up filth about the back-door. There is no better habit for farmer folks to cultivate in regard to poultry than on every occasion to drive them away from the kitchen door, and never to throw out anything that they can eat anywhere near the house. The practice of having a slop-hole—or spot near the back door where dish-water and other "slops," containing more or less that hens will eat, are thrown—is a filthy one at best. All such water should be thrown upon the dung-hill or compost heap. Here the hens may pick up many a crumb, and the manure will be greatly benefited.

In the matter of varieties the fancy breeds are best let alone by any one who does not make a business or a pastime of poultry-keeping. It is very pleasant for a person who keeps but a dozen or twenty hens to have them of some choice breed, and to take great pains with them; studying into their habits, their "points," and all that. But few persons have either the taste or inclination to be successful breeders; so, as a rule, it is best to keep common or mixed hens, but a full-blooded cock of one of the best breeds.

For general use most persons who have had experience will agree that the Plymouth Rock fowls are excellent, and either these or the Dominiques, or one of the Asiatic breeds, are to be recommended if a pure breed of fowls is desired for eggs, broilers, capons, and fat cockerels and pullets. For eggs alone, the White Leghorns are preferable; but they are neither economical for the table, nor are they to be depended upon as sitters and mothers. It is an excellent plan to use full-blooded cocks, making a change, not of cocks alone, but of the breed, every two years. Thus a recent writer, speaking of his own practice, says: "A stock of Light Brahmas were bred with a Dorking cock two years, then with Plymouth Rock cocks, and now I shall probably take a Brahma cross in the hope of effectually eradicating the tendency to throw pink-legged chicks, a relic of the Dorking cross, and black ones, which come from the Plymouth Rocks. After that I shall recur to the last-named variety, as I find it gives me earlier and better broilers, plenty of eggs, and fowls *always* fit for the table."

SALT IN THE RATION FOR POULTRY.

There is a prevalent notion that salt causes the feathers of fowls, or perhaps of the feathered tribes in general, to fall out. This, we believe is well founded. Certainly, excess of this condiment should be avoided. There appears to be some connection between salt and feathers. Feather-eating fowls are often cured of the tendency by adding salt to their food, and a small quantity of salt in the ration promotes, or is supposed to promote, the production of the new crop of feathers at moulting-time. This supposed effect may be simply the loosening of the old feathers. The result, as promotive of moulting, would be the same. Salt is a very important ingredient in the ration of pigeons, and where these birds are confined without it, they are never so thrifty. It is natural, then, to conclude that it is valuable in the food of other birds, and especially for barn-door fowls. The earlier old fowls are out of their moult and in full plumage, the sooner will they begin to lay in the autumn. Pullets usually begin to lay as soon as they are completely plumed as adult fowls. It is worth while, therefore, to encourage moulting in every way, giving them exercise, insect food, or fish in their ration, with ground bone, ground oyster-shell, and sound grain. A tablespoonful of fine salt in the soft feed, given daily to a flock of twenty hens, will be a fair allowance. Fowls do not depend upon this for the salt which their bodies and feathers contain, for either the material itself, or the elements of which it is composed, exist to a greater or less extent in almost all the food they eat and the water they drink; and what we do by giving them salt is simply to increase the supply.

GREEN FOOD FOR FOWLS.

Fowls cannot be kept healthy without a good range, or a supply of green food in their yards. An excellent plan is, to have a roomy yard provided for them, and plant it with plum or dwarf pear trees. Plum-trees are very little troubled by curculios when planted in a chicken-yard, and good crops of fruit are secured, barring accidents of weather at the blooming season. The yard is divided into two parts; one is used for a month, while the other is growing up with some green crop, as turnips, oats, peas, rape, or mustard, which are very acceptable to the fowls. This yard is then used, and the other is plowed and immediately sown. This keeps the ground clean, provides suitable food, and avoids most effectively the troublesome disease known as gapes; the fatal cholera is also evaded by this management; the health being improved, more eggs will be laid.

CHARCOAL AND STIMULANTS.

Poultry in domestication are not in a natural condition. Their diet is more or less restricted in variety, and that which they have is frequently of a character to fatten rather than to promote growth or egg-laying. This may be in a measure counteracted by condimental food or stimulants. Before such measures are taken the poultry-raiser should provide everything else necessary or desirable—grain in variety, broken bones, oyster-shells or other form of lime, green food of some kind, cabbage or roots, gravel, and a dry-dusting box; besides, pure water; and if milk or buttermilk can be had, a trough for that should be provided.

Stimulants must be regarded not as food, but as medicine, used sparingly, and never daily. One mess of stimulating food once in two or three days is enough.

Charcoal should be a stand-by. It defends against disease, keeps up the tone of the system, aids digestion, and promotes laying. Feed it powdered, and mix it up with wheat bran and Indian meal. Add to this mixture a heaping table-spoonful of powdered Cayenne pepper for a dozen fowls, given every third day, or every second day in a cold snap, and continued for about ten days or two weeks, now and again, is promotive of laying and of health. This soft feed may be mixed with hot boiled potatoes, and fed either in the morning or at noon. Besides the hard grain fed at evening regularly, so that the fowls or other poultry may go to roost with full crops, and a little wheat scattered among leaves or straw to make them *scratch* for exercise, they will need little else.

Fig. 60.—GROUP OF BANTAM FOWLS.

SPECIAL FEED CROPS FOR POULTRY.

Every poultry-breeder understands the value of having a variety of food, and that it is essential for the health of the fowls and the production of fertile eggs from which he can expect strong, healthy chickens. One can imagine the result to a community who would try to live exclusively on corn; yet probably nine out of ten who raise poultry think their duty done when they have scattered before them their quart of corn and gathered the eggs. This treatment may appear to fulfill all necessary obligations when fowls can have unrestricted range through the summer season, as nature seems to provide means for sustaining life for feathered as well as human tramps. The necessity of providing corn, sometimes with wheat and oats for winter food, is generally understood; but if to these were added a supply of the other grains and vegetables of which fowls are fond, we would not hear so much complaint as now of stock "running out" and producing nothing but scallions.

As to the special grains, we may name buckwheat as one of the most valuable for the production of eggs. Sunflower-seeds should also be included in the bill of fare of all well-regulated poultry-yards. The large amount of oil they contain seems to be especialy valuable for young, growing chickens. They also give a gloss and brilliancy to the feathers probably unequaled by any other food. Even when fed in large quantities, no bad effects follow, as the husk or shell must be taken with the meat. An experiment was tried, one winter, by an observing poultryman with two flocks, one of five pullets and a cockerel of Plymouth Rocks, the other of twelve pullets and a cock of Light Brahmas, these latter having a well-appointed house, with all of the "modern improvements,"—sunlight, dust-bath, etc.

The former were in a small coop about four feet square, with a covered run formed by throwing cornstalks on some poles, and setting a hot-bed sash up against the south side. The food for the two coops was scalded Indian meal. They were both fed from the same dish, and in proportion according to their numbers. The Plymouth Rocks laid well, and gained in flesh all winter. The Brahmas "went back," both in eggs and in flesh. The reason was that the former had the strippings from the cornstalks to help in the assimilation of their food, which the latter did not have. This proved conclusively that some such coarse food must be provided if we would have the fowls thrive. Well-cured green cornstalks, and young, tender grass and clover should be provided for poultry as regularly as hay for other stock.

The soft or poor heads of cabbages, stored by themselves, probably are the cheapest and most easily obtained green food for poultry during winter. Two or three heads hung so that the fowls can easily reach them, around the sides of their coop, and renewed when necessary, will well repay the trouble. If one is going extensively into the raising of young chickens for an early market, it will pay to sow lettuce-seed in a box, and place it in a warm, sunny window. The young and tender leaves are easily grown, and will add greatly to the health and growth of the chickens. Onions should also be grown and kept for feeding. They are by many considered as a remedy for the chicken-cholera. If chopped moderately fine, they will be eagerly consumed by fowls. Tobacco should also be grown by every poultryman who wishes to keep his stock free from parasitic pests. Pull the plants before frost, and hang them in the barn or shed to dry. A handful of the leaves in the nests of sitting hens, particularly, will add a great deal to their comfort, and more to that of their young. It

Fig. 61.—WHITE SULTAN FOWLS.

(111)

HINTS ABOUT MANAGEMENT.

makes no difference whether the tobacco is ripe or not before pulling. Hemp-seed will be found useful for young and valuable chickens, but the sunflower is a good substitute, and much more cheaply raised. Peppers are a most useful condiment during the winter months, helping greatly in the production of eggs through the cold weather. A small number of plants of the long red variety will produce a plentiful supply, much cheaper and purer than the ordinary ground cayenne of the stores. Use them in connection with potatoes and meal. Set the potatoes on the stove after supper, and boil them until soft. Set them on again when the fire is started in the morning, and bring to a boil; pour off the water, add in one or two chopped pepper-pods, and then add meal, meal and bran, or corn and oats ground together. Mash all together, and make a firm, almost crumbly, mass. This is suitable for a morning meal, but not for night. Beans well cooked, either whole or ground, will help fill up the list of foods. Rape-seed is easily raised, and would be useful for choice young chickens. Seeds of the common millet, golden millet, sorghum, and broom-corn will make a variety in the list of good cheap foods. Egyptian corn, a kind of sorghum, is valuable for young or old fowls. It is raised as easily as corn, and will produce bountifully. Barley, rye, and oats are well known to be acceptable to the inhabitants of the poultry-yard.

WINTERING FOWLS IN COLD LATITUDES.

Extreme care with poultry is necessary in cold latitudes to prevent many frozen feet, and even great loss of life during the cold weather, and it not unfrequently happens that entire flocks are frozen to death. Hence, keeping fowls in winter means simply keeping them alive and well until the spring; eggs are hardly expected.

First, prepare a warm place, well secured from cold winds and shifting snow. A corner in the stable is perhaps best, as the warmth of the stock in the stable is a great help to the chickens. But an independent fowl-house may be made, by digging a cellar, say eight by ten feet, and three feet deep. Build a sod wall three feet thick and five or six feet high around the excavation, with a door in the east and a window in the south side. The window should be double, with one sash at the outside and another on the inside of the wall. Around the door, build an entry or vestibule of sod, with its door opening outward. Plaster all these walls upon the inside. The earth taken from the cellar, mixed with water, will answer to plaster with, and the whole can be done in a short time. The first coat will crack; the second coat should be very thin. The cover or roof may be made of poles and straw. If the poles are strong enough, some earth should be put over the straw, to make the roof warmer. The perches should be made low, and stationary strips arranged, so that the fowls can find their way to the perch, even during the dark, stormy weather. In the second place, the feed must be so arranged that each fowl can both find and eat it in the dark. To secure this end, take a board, one foot wide and four feet long; around this nail four strips three inches wide; two of these strips should be four feet long and the other two fourteen inches long, so as to form a box four feet long by twelve inches wide and two inches deep. Next, cut laths into three equal parts, and nail them perpendicularly around this box two inches apart. Secure the tops by nailing around the outside of a similar board to the bottom, leaving an opening to put in the feed. The feed should always be placed in this box, and the box should always be kept in one position, so it may be as easily found during a storm as on a bright day. Plenty of food, such as the fowls can eat, without seeing it, should always be kept in the box. A vessel of milk-warm water should be set in the box each day, but removed before any ice is formed therein. A wire screen, or one made of slats, may be placed under the perch, to keep the fowls from walking in the droppings, as it is very essential that they keep their feet dry. When the weather is pleasant, let the chickens out into the fresh air awhile each day, but keep them out of the snow. Wheat and screenings may well be kept, say an inch deep, all the time at the bottom of the feed-box, whatever other kind of feed may be given extra.

SELECTING, SELLING, ETC.

Before a fowl is sold, a lot of the best pullets should be picked out, which, with the pullets kept the previous winter, will make up the regular flock. The two-year-old hens should be sold in the spring, as soon as eggs become cheap; they sell better at that time than at any other. A hen has seen her best laying days when she has completed her second year. If eggs are the chief object in view, the cockerels and surplus pullets should be sold as early as possible. The pullets kept for winter layers should be well fed and brought to maturity as rapidly as possible, and they will begin laying in October; and if they are cared for as herein advised, will lay steadily all winter.

EGGS IN WINTER.

Winter is the very time when eggs are worth the most, when hens want to lay as much or more than they do at any other time, and when they are not allowed to do so by most poultry-keepers. Folks think there is a great mystery about making hens lay in winter. There is none; anybody can do it; that is, the hens will lay if you let them. They bear a good deal of cold in the sunshine, and even freeze their combs and toes, and yet will not stop laying altogether if they can sleep warm. Now do not begin to plan setting up a stove in the henhouse, or introducing steam-pipes. Artificial heat is not poisonous perhaps, but very nearly so, to chickens. They are warm themselves, and need only to be crowded on their roosts, with the roosts all on one level. The ceiling of the roosting-room should be only a few feet above the fowls' heads, and provided with ventilation from the floor if possible. Give them very close quarters, with no draughts of cold air, and clean out under the roosts every morning, not excepting Sundays. The combs will then redden up, and eggs will be plenty on less feed than usual. It must not be corn, however, or only a small percentage of it, for this will make them too fat to lay well if they sleep warm.

A capital way to arrange a hen-house for winter is to make a ceiling of rails about six feet above the floor, covering the rails with salt hay, or coarse swamp hay of any kind. The roosts should be about three feet high above the floor, and movable, so that they may be kept perfectly clean. For small flocks of thirty to fifty hens, it is little trouble to take the roosts down every morning when the floor is cleaned, and replace them at night. It removes from lazy fowls the temptation to sit in idleness on the roost for half the day.

PREVENTION AGAINST LICE.

Almost all poultry are lousy, more or less. "A. B." says: good arrangements for dusting will always keep the lice in check. The small hen louse moves along the roosts and sides of the building several feet, and sometimes annoys cattle and horses, but the trouble to them is quite temporary. If the fowls are free from them, they will leave other stock at once. Roosts ought always to be removable, so that they can be scraped and washed with kerosene. I find kerosene or crude petroleum an excellent addition to whitewash. This treatment, with a good dusting-box for the fowls, in which there may be occasionally thrown a pailful of wood ashes and a pound of flowers of sulphur, will keep lice effectually in check. Horses and cattle in adjoining apartments, with only loose board partitions separating them from the poultry-house, will not be seriously troubled by the vermin.

A POULTRYMAN'S CROOK.

J. L. Cunningham, Gonzales Co., Texas, writes us: It is often troublesome to catch one out of a number of fowls in a coop. To save time and labor in such a case, I make use of an instrument like the one here figured. A small rod, three fourths of an inch in diam-

Fig. 61.—HOOK FOR CATCHING POULTRY.

eter and three or four feet long, is provided with a ferrule at one end. A stout, medium-sized wire, about one foot long, is bent at one end, and the long end of the wire inserted firmly into the ferruled end of the rod. Then by reaching into the coop of fowls with the rod, the one desired may be caught by the foot, and gently drawn within reach. I do not think the above invention has ever been patented, and it is too good to keep. By its use one person may handle a coop of fowls, which without it would require at least two or three persons to accomplish.

PASTURING POULTRY.

The farmer whose acres are broad can enclose his garden with a fence, and let the poultry run at will, but villagers and suburban residents, living on small lots, must enclose their chickens if they desire to cultivate either a garden or the good will of their neighbors. During the spring and summer months it is necessary that chickens have a supply of fresh, tender, green food, if kept in a healthy, growing condition. They cannot eat grass when it is tall enough to mow, and the refuse of the garden is little better than husks. A good plan is to pasture the chickens. Make a wire cage, put it on wheels having flanges, lay a track for the wheels to run on, and sow oats between. The frame is three feet high, six feet wide, and eight long. The upper part is 2 by 2-inch pine; the sills 2 by 4 inches. The wheels are sawed from 2-inch oak plank, and turn on 1-inch bolts. The flanges are 1-inch stuff, nailed to the wheels. The track is 2 by 2-inch stuff laid on the ground, the strips being thrown on top as the cage passes along. Wire half the thickness of fence wire is strong enough. The soil between the rails should be worked over, and sown with oats early in the spring and in successive sowings. When an inch high it will do to pasture. Have a small door in the poultry yard to match the one in the cage. Half an hour's pasturing each day will do the chickens more good than any amount of green stuff thrown to them. When the crop seems exhausted, let the fowls scratch it over; then sow again.

HINTS ABOUT MANAGEMENT.

HOW TO GET LARGE BIRDS.

Many purchasers of fine stock, or of their immediate descendants, fail to secure as fine birds as the seller raises, and are unhappy. They hear of eighteen-pound light or dark Brahma cocks, and twelve-pound hens of some noted breeder, or of mammoth bronze turkeys weighing sixty or more pounds to the pair. They order the eggs or young birds of such stock, hand them over to some servant or neighbor, who is not skilled in breeding, feeds irregularly, or regularly stints them, and at the end of six months wonder that they have not first-class birds, equal to the advertisement. They think they have been cheated, and set down the breeder as a rogue. There are men, no doubt, in the poultry business who cannot be trusted, but there are also a large number of men who have brought capital, skill, and integrity to their business, and who would not knowingly let a poor fowl go from their yards. They sell, uniformly, stock true to name, but at so early an age that the development does not always answer expectations. A turkey does not get its full growth until the third year, but most of them are sold at from four to eight months. Ducks and hens are not fully developed until the second year, and yet most of them are sold under nine months old. While it is true that large stock is essential to the raising of large birds, another factor is quite as essential. This is abundant feed during the whole period of growth. The grand results obtained by our skillful breeders are reached by care and feed, after they have selected their stock. To make the most of a young bird, it should be fed with a variety of food at least five times a day, from daylight in the morning until the middle of the afternoon. It is well to omit late feeding, to give time for digestion. Slack or full feed will make a difference of six pounds in the weight of a turkey-gobbler at eight months old, which is the most of the difference between an ordinary and an extraordinary bird. Persons who buy thoroughbred young birds of good breeders should not expect to buy the skill of the breeder with his stock. That is a commodity that cannot be bought for money. It can only be gained by daily attention to the details of poultry breeding.

CHAPTER XIII.

SOME POPULAR BREEDS.

The agricultural interest owes much to poultry-fanciers. Those who devote their attention to fancy poultry are too often misunderstood by farmers as well as by others. As in many other cases where people devote themselves to some special pursuit—or hobby, as it is considered—the poultry-fanciers are generally looked upon as enthusiasts, who simply amuse themselves, without conferring any benefit upon the public; an error which does the poultry-breeder great injustice. In nearly every farmer's yard may be seen either some pure-bred or some crossed fowls that are much superior to the ordinary run of "barn-door" poultry. The common fowls may weigh three pounds at maturity, and may lay two or three dozen of eggs in the summer, and none in the winter. But the improved fowls, now kept by the majority of farmers, will reach an average weight of four pounds, and produce eggs, if not in the winter, at least very early in the spring, and continue late in the fall. The product of flesh and eggs is at least doubled. This result is due to the labors of poultry-fanciers, who have ransacked the world for new varieties, until perhaps there are none worth having that are not now to be found in this country.

No one can become a successful breeder of poultry—indeed one can hardly succeed in anything—unless he is an enthusiast; therefore enthusiasm, when usefully directed, is something to be commended rather than blamed. The profit derived by small farmers from poultry is usually an important item in their income.

We therefore advocate the improvement of poultry

by encouraging those who make it the business of their lives.

It is especially advisable that farmers should at least procure pure-bred cocks or cockerels for breeders, yet such a thing is the exception rather than the rule. In regard to this matter, Mr. Evans says: Many of the farmers can readily realize that it pays to use pure-bred bulls, or pure-bred rams, or pure-bred boars in their herds and flocks of cows, sheep, and swine; but they do not seem to realize that the same rule holds good with poultry, and also that the benefits are secured very quickly. This infusion of pure-bred blood amongst a flock of good common hens is sure to be of great benefit, as the constitutional vigor of the common stock intensifies the good qualities derived from the thoroughbreds, producing in point of early maturity, size, and laying qualities something both desirable and profitable, though these half-bloods cannot with anything like uniformity transmit these improved qualities to their offspring. First-class pure-bred cockerels can be bought at a moderate figure, and we do not see how farmers can afford to use the common ones in preference, no matter how good they may be. If large size is most desired, the Asiatics will be found to answer well, while for laying qualities principally we commend the Leghorns.

The popular breeds of the day may be classed among either the Asiatic, European, or American varieties.

CHAPTER XIV.

ASIATIC BREEDS.

The Brahmas, Cochins, and Langshans, which comprise the standard Asiatic breeds, have many desirable qualities. They are docile, not mischievous; fair layers, persistent sitters, and good mothers. As a class, there is little difference between the varieties; what may be said of one will generally apply to the others, the color of plumage being the chief point of preference that decides a choice.

LIGHT BRAHMAS.

The Light Brahma is now well known amongst breeders and fanciers, but is not yet nearly so popular amongst farmers, and those who rear poultry for market, as it should be. The small head, the lofty carriage, the broad full breast, the deep round body, the short, stout, well-feathered legs,—all mark the high-bred bird, and one producing a great amount of flesh with the least offal. This is one distinguishing feature of the Brahma fowl which renders it a profitable breed for the farmer. No other bird excels it as a winter layer; and as it is a good mother, the plentiful fluff about it serving to keep the chicks warm in the coldest weather, and as the chicks are hardy, it is easy to have very early birds. The young birds, as broilers, are remarkably juicy, well-flavored, and tender; and the young cockerels of four to six months, weighing, as they easily do, six to eight pounds, make most excellent roasters. As with all high-bred, pure races, the half-breed crosses of these, upon common stock, are nearly as good as the pure breed. To introduce one young cock for every twenty-five common hens would be to easily double the value of the farmer's yearly product.

From the time of its first introduction to American poultry-breeders, the breed has been held in the highest esteem. Other varieties have come up, the Plymouth Rock and Wyandottes, as market birds, and Leghorns in variety as egg-producers; still the Light Brahma has held its own as a family fowl among the lovers of choice poultry. Although quiet and unassuming in style, it has great dignity of carriage, and is really a majestic fowl. In excellent qualities for family use, it is hardly approached by any other. Its flesh is juicy and tender; and as it puts on flesh very fast, it remains a "chicken" until fully grown. The excellence of the hens as layers depends greatly on how they were bred, for some families are extraordinary egg-producers taken in comparison with other large-bodied fowls. They are layers of large, buff-colored eggs, which are very rich, and great favorites in the market. In disposition they are very kind and quiet. An ordinary picket-fence, three feet high, will restrain them; and if handled gently, they can be picked up at any time. The plumage is white with black points. The tail is black, as are also the flight feathers of the wings, which are not discernible when the wings are folded. There is also a fine penciling of black in the neck. It has a "pea," or triple comb, which, being small and set close to the head, is proof against all ordinary frost. They are easy to rear, very hardy, quick growers, and make very heavy fowls. On a well-kept lawn, there is nothing handsomer than a flock of Light Brahmas.

It is an interesting fact in connection with this breed that it is the only one of the Asiatic breeds not received through England. The original birds were brought

Fig. 62.—LIGHT BRAHMA COCK.

by a sailor to New York, obtained by a Connecticut breeder, the late Virgil Cornish of Hartford, bred and brought out by him.

DARK BRAHMAS.

In an article which recently appeared in a poultry journal, the writer says: " But few of the breeders are aware of the fact that this beautiful breed was perfected in the hands of our English breeders, out of a brood of chickens that were bred by mating a Black-red Shanghai cock with a Gray Shanghai (or, as then called, Chitegong) hen. But this is the fact. They were sent to England by an American breeder.

"There was no more heard from them, and the word Dark Brahmas, as a distinct breed of fowls, was not known in America till 1865, when the first importation was made. The assertion that the Dark and Light Brahmas were bred from the same original stock without crossing is not true. The first imported ones came with far more single-combs than Pea-combs. The breeding of Pea Comb Brahmas to Partridge Cochins produced new blood; and later we began to get them of less Cochin shape and in every way improved. Such was the early history of the breed.

"It is not a very flattering thought for home industry that we must send the crude material to a foreign country to be woven into a web of cloth, or perfected into a breed, and receive the same as a thoroughbred in only about a dozen years afterward. Be that as it may, our English brothers in this case have made for us a fine breed, and deserve much praise, and I for one would acknowledge the worth, and give the credit where it belongs.

"The earlier specimens were, more or less, bronzed

in the wing-coloring of the cocks, and the females bronze-gray in the ground-color, breeding more closely to the Partridge Cochin; but the introduction of Light Brahma cocks as an occasional cross secured the steel-gray color, which has become the standard color of America. These crosses have been so frequent that the reversion in color is prone to light, and we find English breeders indulging in the use of Partridge Cochin hens, occasionally, to retain the distinct barring of the feather in the females.

"My taste and knowledge of the breeds lead me to say that next to the Light Brahmas, among the Asiatics, the Dark Brahma must take rank in merit; yet I am compelled to acknowledge that the breed is fourth in the taste and demand of the public."

THE COCHINS.

The Cochin breed of fowls was introduced into this country about the year 1847, and to this was mainly due the celebrated "poultry mania" long to be remembered by breeders of domestic fowls. Men became almost wild after Partridge Cochins, and were willing to spend a small fortune for a trio of fine birds. The neck-hackles of the hens are bright gold, striped with black, the rest of the body being light brown, penciled with a darker shade of the same color. The hackles of the Partridge Cochin cock are bright-red, striped with black, the back being dark-red, with a bar of metallic green upon the wings. The breast and under part of the body are pure black. Some of the points of merit, as claimed by the breeders of these fowls, are as follows: they are hardier than any other breeds, except the Brahmas, and will thrive under conditions where most others would perish.

Fig. 63.—GROUP OF LIGHT BRAHMAS.

(129)

ASIATIC BREEDS.

They are of large size, with a very gentle disposition, and the ease with which the Cochins are kept in confinement makes them favorites with many poultry-raisers. When full-grown the weight ranges from ten to fifteen pounds; they are too heavy to fly, and a fence two feet high will confine them. As sitters and mothers the hens are not surpassed, and are prolific layers, especially in winter, when eggs are scarce. The chickens grow rapidly, and at three months are large enough for eating.

It is true, they have some defects. The flesh is inferior, especially of old birds. The inclination to sit sometimes interferes with their greatest usefulness. This tendency is developed by over-feeding. As a breed the Cochins are most useful to supply the demands of a family for early chickens and a plenty of large, rich eggs. If the Cochins had done nothing more than to awaken a general interest in poultry-breeding, their introduction would still have been of benefit.

Besides the Partridge, which may be either of the single or Pea-comb variety, the principal sub-varieties of the Cochins are the White, Buff, and Black. With those who breed the White variety every feather must be pure, otherwise the fowl is looked upon with disfavor. The Buff Cochins may be of any shade, but the birds in a flock must correspond in color. With the Blacks, it is of the utmost importance that every feather should be solid black. In other respects than plumage, the several varieties of Cochins are very similar.

THE LANGSHAN FOWLS.

The Langshans are natives of the extreme northern part of China, where most of the fowls, both wild and domestic, are black, and where the winters are very severe. Mr. C. W. Gedney, of Bromley, Kent, England, resided for some years in that country, and professes to be well acquainted with the habits and character of these fowls, and we depend upon him for most of the information we have in regard to them in their native

Fig. 64.—LANGSHAN COCK.

country. They are entirely distinct from the Black Cochin, and their native home is 1000 miles distant from Cochin-China, whence the latter birds have been brought. These birds are erect in carriage, have larger combs, more feathered tails than the Black Cochins, **and**

Fig. 65.—PAIR OF BUFF COCHINS.

are more active, hardy, and vigorous. A cockerel of this breed, seven months old, will weigh, if fattened, ten to twelve pounds; and a pullet of the same age, eight to nine pounds; the flesh is well-flavored and tender, and thickly laid upon the breast, the skin is clear white and transparent, and the bone very light and fine. The legs are of a bright slate color, and pink between the toes, and the plumage black with a vivid beetle-green reflection. These birds were first introduced into England in 1872 by an officer of the British army, Major Croad, of Sussex, who received them directly from a relative living in the northern part of China. Since then a second importation has been received in England, and Mr. Gedney states that the breed has been used to improve the Black Cochins. Since the opening of the Suez Canal, by which the voyage from China has been much shortened, the importation of fowls from that distant part of the world has been rendered much easier. Mr. Gedney sums up the merits of these fowls as follows: Extreme hardiness, rapid growth, great size combined with small bone, exquisitely white skin and flesh of the same purity of color, full breast, delicacy of flavor, and possessing none of that dryness so common to most of the large breeds. As prolific winter layers of large rich eggs, the Langshan hens will hold their own against all comers, whilst they lack that intense desire to sit which is so essentially a characteristic of the Cochin. In short, he considers that they "are the finest and most practically useful birds ever brought to England."

The Langshans were admitted to the American Standard of Excellence by the American Poultry Association at the meeting held at Worcester, Mass., 1883.

CHAPTER XV.

EUROPEAN BREEDS.

DORKINGS.

Speaking of this breed, a well-known authority says: Looking back into the dim past, to find any record of any pure-bred fowls is almost useless. But few peculiarities were noted in ancient records; perhaps the Dorking and Polish fowls are the only ones that can claim any great antiquity. In ancient paintings hens with crests are often seen resembling our Polish birds, and from which the latter are probably descended; and Columella, an old Roman writer, gives directions for the selecting of poultry to breed from, "such as five claws, square frames," etc. Such birds have been bred in England for centuries, but varying in color; the probability is that they were imported by the Romans while Britain was a Roman colony, for they took most of their luxuries along with them. At any rate, these fowls have been so long known in England that they are called an English breed; they have been bred mottled, gray, splashed, cuckoo or dominique colored, white, and silver-gray, which is the last fashion in color.

A fine Silver-gray Dorking cock is a well-shaped, noble bird, of about eight or nine pounds weight, with full silver hackle and graceful flowing tail; he certainly makes a show that few birds can match; his face and comb are bright-red, beak strongly arched; saddle, back, and hackle fine silvery white, wing coverts the same; breast, thighs, and tail black when complying with the Standard, but the thighs of young birds are nearly always a little grayish if the bird is any *size*, and birds over one or two years old with me invariably have a little white on sickles. I have corresponded with many breeders of this breed, and they invariably tell the same experience. In "Lewis Wright's Illustrated Poultry Book,"

Fig. 66.—WHITE DORKING FOWLS.

the only portrait of a Silver-gray Dorking cock, which took cups at Crystal Palace, 1871; Dublin. 1872, and at all the principal English shows, has a white edge to the lower half of his sickle tail feathers. Hon. W. F.

Daniels, N. H., who carried the palm for his celebrated birds, states that he never had a bird worth breeding from that did not show white in his sickles at two years old; such birds are liable to be marked disqualified at any fair, as is sometimes done by judges who never kept and never knew anything about Dorkings, except from the Standard. The hen is a finely penciled steel-gray on back shoulders, and lower back part of body; the shafts of feathers on back form a fine white line, breast clear salmon color or light robin-red, shafts of feathers a lighter shade. The feet and legs of the hens, and also of

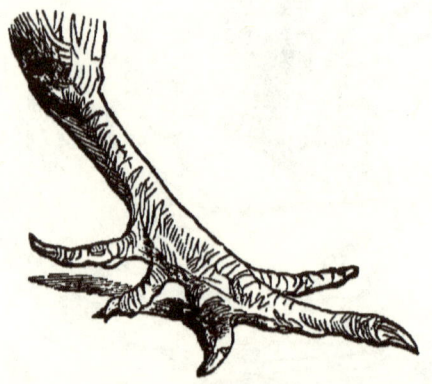

Fig. 67.—FOOT OF DORKING FOWL.

the cocks, pink or flesh colored, with five distinct toes, the fifth or upper toe well separated from the others, and slightly turned up. The neck is of a fine silvery-white color, with a black stripe down each feather. The disposition of this breed is very docile; no breed shows more intelligence; they are the best of mothers, taking care of their chicks for a much longer time than most fowls; they are good layers of fair-sized eggs, and lay well all through the summer; if not the best of winter layers, they commence early and keep it up till late in the season. One great advantage of this breed is, they are in their prime when most fowls are too old for use; they are long-lived. A hen has been known to bring up two broods in a season when she was six years old. They are most remarkable as foragers, being very active, industrious workers; if they do not improve your garden, they will find a good deal of their food on a farm or good run. As table fowl, their praises have been often sounded. They are second to none, and their cross with game produces a table fowl of absolutely supreme merit.

GAME FOWLS.

While the Asiatic, Leghorns, Hamburgs, Polands, and a host of other breeds, each have their champion advocates, each claiming for their particular favorites all the profitable good qualities, there are but few who advocate the cause of the Game fowl, and really but few who fully understand the superior qualities of this *Royal Bird.* The origin and nationality of the Game fowl have always been, and yet remain, a mooted question.

The record of Game fowls is as old as the oldest written history, wherein we find that the Persians, Greeks, Romans, and a host of other nations, each had their native Game fowls.

Games were known to the Britons, and cock-fighting was carried on in England prior to Cæsar's invasion, and hundreds of years prior to the Christian era, cock-fighting was an established insititution with the Greeks and Persians. China, Java, and the entire East Indies each had their native Game fowls.

Therefore, all theories advanced by naturalists as to the origin of the Game fowl are wholly speculative.

The Game fowl was regarded as sacred to the *gods* in ancient times, and was used in ancient military schools for teaching the youth, by practical illustration, courage and endurance in battle. They were used as emblems of ancient nationalities, being stamped on war banners, coins and shields; and, having withstood the decline of empires and witnessed the rise and fall of nations, they yet maintain to the present time their fame for gameness as of old, and are emphatically the kings of all domestic fowls.

But not alone for their antiquity and historic glory do the Game fowls stand at the head of their kind, as they possess useful qualities in a very high degree, being good layers of good-sized eggs, and the most devoted of mothers.

THE DUCK-WINGED GAME.

Of the varieties of Game fowls the Duck-winged is one of the most beautiful. Although its graceful form and dignified carriage are exceedingly attractive, its brilliantly colored plumage is still more so, and can only be truly shown by the painter's art. Its bright and varied colors are so beautifully blended together that it excites the admiration of those even who take no delight in breeding poultry, while to the fancier it is one of the first favorites. The face of the Duck-wing Game is a deep crimson; the head is covered with small silvery-white feathers; the hackle is white, slightly tinged with straw-yellow; the back is maroon, claret and straw-yellow; the saddle is slightly darker than the hackle, with fine short feathers hiding the points of the wings; the shoulders are bright brass-yellow from the butts up to the clear steel bar, and no light streak is admissible in a well-bred bird; the shoulder butts are black; the breast and tail are black, with a shade of bronze upon the sickle feathers; the eyes are red, and the legs yellow. The

Fig. 68.—BLACK-BREASTED RED GAME-COCK.

(141)

weight is from five to six pounds. The hen, when pure bred, has the head gray; comb and face bright red; hackle silvery gray, with dark stripes; the breast is bright salmon-red; the back and shoulder coverts should be slaty-gray, free from penciling; the tail is dark gray, so dark as to be nearly black; the fluff inside is a steel gray, and the legs yellow. In breeding Duck-wings for color, much care and skill is necessary; for the ordinary uses of poultry it is not necessary to do more than select the best birds, feed well, and keep them in the best and most vigorous health. Unfortunately for game poultry, their courage and endurance has been put to wrong uses, and through their enforced connection with the brutal and cruel sports of the cock-pit, they have in a measure come to be identified therewith, and are wrongly supposed to be good for nothing but fighting. On the contrary, the Game fowl is one of the most, if not the most, beautiful of our fowls. It is the best table fowl, so far as regards quality and flavor of flesh. Its eggs are exceedingly rich, and much desired for pastry or cakes. The cock is courageous, and will not hesitate to attack the hawk, and will defeat the intruder in every attempt to ravage the poultry yard. The hen is an excellent mother, and although somewhat nervous and excitable when brooding her chickens, yet with care and quiet, gentle treatment she may be handled with ease. While brooding, she is as courageous as the cock, and will defend her chickens from a hawk, and generally with success. A farmer whose grain fields, and those of his neighbors, offer a too tempting foraging ground for these active fowls, would be wise to choose some of the heavier bodied breeds; but where no damage of this kind can occur, any of the varieties of Game fowls might be chosen by those who fancy them, and wish for delicious eggs and flesh.

GAME FOWLS—A SENSIBLE GROWL.

It is a noticeable fact that the department of Games in our poultry exhibitions is the great center of attraction. Game fowls command higher prices than any of the old varieties, the eggs sell higher, and they are more extensively advertised in the poultry journals. The secret of this popularity lies mainly in the use to which these birds are put. The Game is unquestionably a good bird for eating, but is no better than some of the less quarrelsome varieties. They are prolific, but are surpassed by other varieties. They are quite handsome, but this is not what they are bred for. The only thing in which they excel all other domestic fowls is their capacity to fight until the last gasp. No doubt many breed them for their flesh and eggs. They are frequently crossed with other fowls, but their quarrelsome disposition does not make them favorites with the poultry-men, who only want flesh and eggs. They are mostly bred for the pit, and there is unquesionably an increasing love of this cruel sport, principally among a certain class in our cities and villages. Cock fights are common, held in some places on the sly, in other places quite openly, and attended by the same rabble that run after prize fights in the ring, and for the same reason. They show courage, and draw blood, and offer opportunities for betting and gambling. Frequently a main is fought, and several cocks are pitted against a similar number upon the other side. It is expected in these contests that all the cocks upon one side will be killed. The worst passions are stirred by these brute contests, and there is the same objection to them that there is to other forms of gambling. The bull fights of Spain are no more bloody and cruel. They tend to harden the sensibilities, and so corrupt the morals. All the associations are low and degrading. There may be laws against these contests in some of the States, but they are seldom enforced, and do not remedy the evil. Our poultry societies have some responsibility in fostering the breeding of these birds. As a matter of fact, we think most of them would be found obnoxious to the charge of discriminating in their favor, instead of encouraging the more useful and ornamental varieties. With the single exception of the Asiatic fowls, the largest amount of premiums is generally offered for Games. The premiums for turkeys, the most valuable of all our domestic birds, amount to much less. For geese, still less. Now, if the object of these societies is the promotion of the common weal, the highest premiums should be offered for the birds that are most useful, or for those that promise to be such. The managers should so arrange the list of premiums as to draw out the birds that will be the most profitable on the farm and in the poultry yard. No special inducements are needed for the breeding of Game fowls. That business would take care of itself if the premiums were altogether diverted to the most useful classes.

HAMBURGS.

In writing of Hamburgs, an admirer of this favorite breed says: They have taken their proper place in the list of popular breeds. All varieties of the Hamburg family are beautiful, symmetrical, and stylish in carriage. They have been much improved in the beauty and uniformity of plumage since the era of poultry exhibits, but not in productiveness, as that is hardly possible; for they have long maintained the reputation of being "every-day layers." Birds of the Hamburg family are of only medium size, but their deficiency in size is more than made up for by their fecundity. Both sexes exhibit such glossy and elegantly marked plumage that they are looked upon as special favorites wherever shown or cultivated, and when well-bred are truly ornamental, possessing fancy points that render them pleasing to those who desire to keep pets that will furnish plenty of eggs and also be a gratification to the eye.

Our standard recognizes six varieties of the Hamburg breed,—the Black, Silver-penciled, Golden-penciled, Silver-spangled, Golden-spangled, and White. The

Fig. 69.—SILVER-SPANGLED HAMBURGS.

whole family is remarkably attractive in plumage, capital appendages, and the graceful curves which mark the outline of their well-rounded forms. In sprightliness, carriage, and habits they are much alike. The Black is a trifle larger and in appearance stouter than any of the other varieties.

For table use, though small, they are very good; their flesh is tender, with little offal, having a larger proportion than usual of the dressed weight in flesh, from the delicate structure of the skeleton, and is fine in quality.

Fig. 70.—GROUP OF POLISH FOWLS.

(147)

The cocks average about five pounds, and the hens four pounds. They will always be prime favorites with a large class of fanciers and village poultry-raisers.

THE POLISH FOWL.

There are several varieties of these ornamental fowls, differing but little except in their plumage. The main characteristics of each are alike, all being non-sitters, and are by many called everlasting layers. As a class, they are very prolific, and easily raised, feathering out and coming to maturity early. They are small compared with many varieties, but when full-grown weigh from ten to twelve pounds per pair. They are remarkably handsome, and in the yard or lawn have few superiors in beauty. In rearing them tastes differ; some prefer the White-crested Black, others the White and Spangled varieties. They are distinguished by a crest crowning the head, which gives them the appearance of a field-marshal in plumes, though in illustrations this feature is somewhat over-drawn. They are especially adapted to city residences, the lawn, and small inclosures, and extremely domestic in their habits. They seem fond of attention, and become remarkably tame and fond of the society of their keeper; are a hardy breed to raise, but sensitive to cold and wet; require warm, dry quarters, their heavy topknots hanging so far over their eyes as to interfere with their sight. They lay a large white egg of oblong shape, very creamy and rich, and for culinary uses is among the best quality. But the peculiar merit consists in their tame and quiet dispositions and fondness of attention, their extremely ornamental appearance on the lawn, graceful carriage, and the glossy and metallic lustre of their plumage. They are quite liable to pick each other's crests, and while in this condition render the top of the head bare and disfigured. Their coops should be kept clean, and feed supplied them regularly, as they are poor foragers, and little inclined to scratch and wander. Never sitting, they must be raised by other hens; and when first hatched a brood of the White-crested Black look like a line of diminutive grenadiers with white caps. Several gentlemen have turned special attention to improving this family and restoring them to their original purity, and by careful breeding are producing specimens that command the admiration of all. For many reasons we regard the Black and White Polish as the most fascinating and desirable breed of fowls for the young amateur to handle, always observing our standing admonition with this as with all other varieties, to breed but one strain, and that as nearly perfect as possible. If your taste fixes upon the White-crested Black, take that and breed for beauty; or upon the White or Golden, give that your best care. Whichever variety you select, give that your special culture. There is no variety that so quickly develops the error of a cross and disfigurement of a mixture as either variety of Polands, and when carefully and purely bred we know of none giving more pleasure and satisfaction to the breeder, or that can approach them in beauty as ornamental appendages to the yards and lawns of a city or suburban residence, and winning the attention and praise of our most prominent fanciers of pets, while as egg-producers they are not easily excelled.

WHITE-CRESTED WHITE POLISH FOWLS.

The origin of crested fowls is somewhat obscure. Cuvier and Buffon mention them, but are unable to fix upon their original source. It is supposed that they

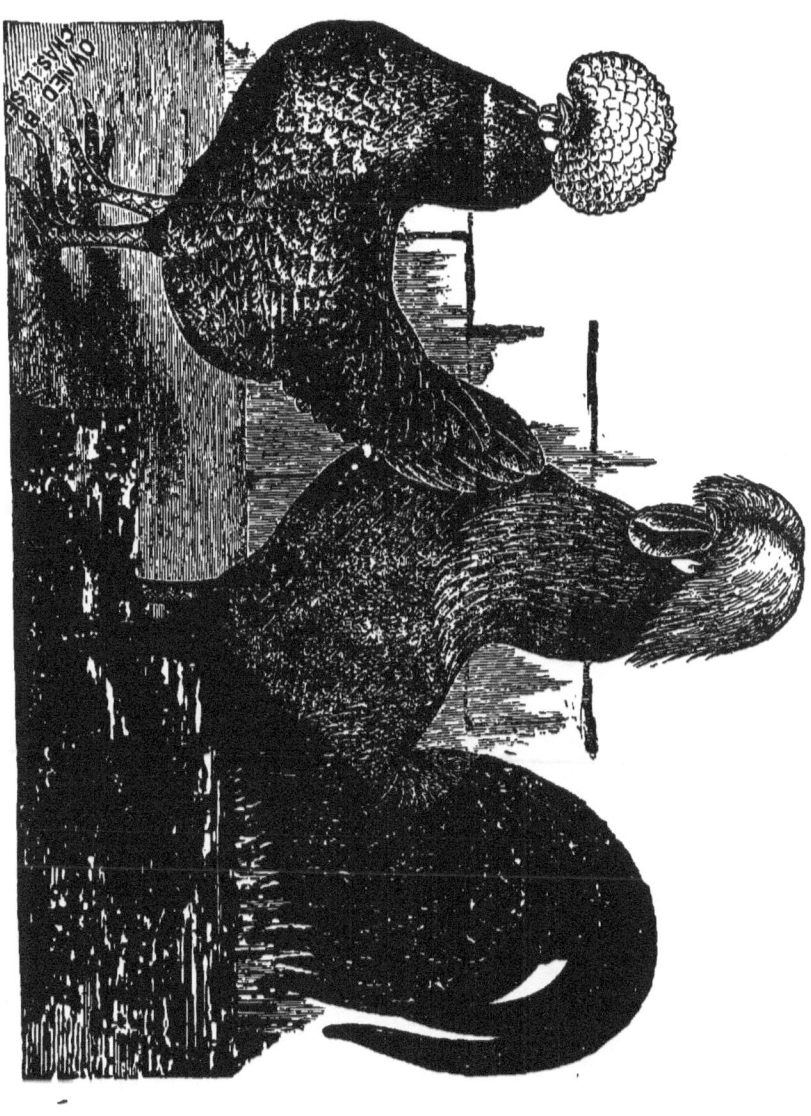

Fig. 71.—WHITE-CRESTED BLACK POLISH FOWLS.

(151)

were first described by an Italian author, about 260 years ago, in whose treatise rough wood-cuts of some crested fowls were given as "Paduan Fowls." Paduan was an Italian city, and these crested fowls were, therefore, Italian. Buffon refers to the Paduan fowls, and supposed them to have been descended from Asiatic stock; he also described a variety with white body and black crest, which has long been extinct, although breeders have made many efforts to restore it. The vareties of the Polish fowls now known are the White-crested White, the White-crested Black, the Golden, and the Silver-spangled, with some bearded varieties. Of these the most beautiful is, perhaps, the first mentioned. The Polish fowls are profuse layers, non-sitters, delicate table fowls, of handsome appearance; they possess an oddity in their crests, which makes them attractive to the fancier and the amateur. They are contented in confinement, and bear close quarters very well; are easily kept within bounds and, becoming readily attached to their owners, make pleasing pets. When young, they are unusually elegant with their full crests, gracefully shaped little bodies, and tame disposition. On the whole, there is hardly any other breed which would give more satisfactory results in every way, where but one is kept, than this. For ornament, the pure white breeds have a decided advantage over the colored ones, because they show so conspicuously upon a green lawn or a field. The White Leghorn is very popular on this account, as well as for its prolific egg-producing; but the White Polish has an advantage over the graceful Leghorn in the possession of a crest, a heavier body, and better flesh, as well as being equally valuable as an egg-producer. For ornament, therefore, as well as for use, the White Polish should be popular fowls.

THE BLACK SPANISH FOWL.

Doubtless there exists no breed of thoroughbred fowls in any country, except the Game, which can lay claim to priority of origin or to such an unbroken line of pure lineage as the Black Spanish. Nearly two thousand years ago Columella wrote about them; they were then indigenous to Spain, and not generally known in the Roman Empire. Faint traces of their origin to the Phœnician colony of Carthage, through the doubtful media of Celtic poetry, are not sufficiently reliable of themselves to substantiate the claim.

The Black Spanish is possibly the fourth in the order of Gallinæ, or, in other words, the fourth distinct variety of the *Gallus bankiva*. Time has effected but little change in them during those years of close breeding. The same vital element, the same stamina, and the same power of reproducing their like in plumage, contour, symmetry, carriage, and facial markings are as characteristic of the breed to-day as they were of them in past centuries. Some writers assert several varieties of the Black Spanish, as the Minorca, Red-faced, Black, the White, the Blue, Andalusian, and the Gray or Mottled Ancona. Although each of these varieties was produced by the amalgamation of the Black Spanish with other provincial breeds, yet, strictly speaking, each is definitely classed by the best-informed Spanish breeders as distinct varieties, inasmuch as they belong to the Mediterranean islands and provinces of Spain. Their resemblance to the Spanish is indeed close. Affinity no doubt exists; but nowadays, when skillful discriminations, careful selections, and thorough breeding produce those nice and fine points not found in the original congenitors, the progeny in time assumes distinctive features, plumage, and peculiar characteristics, so as to be considered a distinct variety of breed. The white face on the Spanish is purely Castilian, and it is a mooted question whether this feature is natural or was produced by years of study and skillful cultivation.

Fig. 72.—WHITE-FACED BLACK SPANISH COCK.

The feathering of the Spanish is close and hard. The metallic lustre which tips the hackle, back, and wings contrasts beautifully with the white face, bright-red comb and wattles.

The carriage of the cock should combine stateliness, alertness, and gracefulness; he should be proud and carry his breast full and projecting; his color should be jet-black; white or partially white feathers is a serious fault; the comb, single and extending from the fore part of the nostrils in an arched form. The white face is the most important feature. It should be pure white, rising well over the eye and extending to the back of the head, covering the deep-sided cheeks, and jointing the long and well-rounded white ear-lobes and thin wattles.

The Black Spanish are great layers; none surpass them in beauty, nor excel them in size and quantity of eggs. Our northern winters are too severe for them; yet they seem to do well, if we judge by the grand display of our poultry exhibitions. They require great care during chickenhood; cold rains, damp houses and runs, and close confinement are positive seeds of mortality. They love to roam over the ample grounds of the breeder's homestead, where they can bask in sunshine and display their unique and ornamental facial markings.

WHITE AND BROWN LEGHORNS.

The Leghorns have been widely known in this country for the last twenty years. They have been growing in public favor every year, until they now stand in the first rank of pure-bred poultry. They did not spring up in a few years to their present standing and popularity, but with steady strides have gained hosts of admirers among both veteran and amateur fowl-breeders for their remarkable precocity and productiveness.

Without doubt, we have no variety of domestic fowls among the improved breeds at present cultivated in this country that will during the year produce a larger num-

Fig. 78.—PAIR OF WHITE LEGHORNS.

ber of eggs on the average than the Leghorn. The laying of eggs is their great forte; and if they be properly cared for and fed, they will lay well through cold weather, the hens being powerful machines for converting food into eggs.

The Leghorns, on a good range, can pick up the greater part of their own living. They are the most active and industrious foragers known. But if one is obliged to confine them to a small yard, clip their wing primaries to keep them within bounds, and you will be surprised to see how they will scratch and keep busy day after day.

It is true there is some trouble experienced in wintering Leghorns successfully in our frigid climate; so that they will appear at our annual shows and come out in spring with their combs and pendants unscathed by Jack Frost. But, as it often has been said by our leading fanciers of this and other high-combed varieties, they should be kept in quarters where there is no danger of freezing; and no poultryman who values his fowls should allow them in winter to occupy a place that is not warm and comfortable.

From the time Leghorns leave the shell they grow rapidly, are hardy, active, strong, and healthy, mature early, and are comparatively free from disease. During moulting, when other breeds succumb to the drain on the system by shedding and putting on their coat of feathers, they take on their new plumage quickly, and show little signs of weakness or debility.

They are a proud, sprightly, and handsome variety of fowls. They are singularly precocious, and it is quite common to see the pullets developed and doing their duty as layers before they have attained the age of five months; and the cockerels—such little scamps—making love before they are four months old.

The general objection to the Whites is the difficulty in keeping the plumage unsoiled. Where, however, they receive proper care there is little trouble.

BROWN LEGHORN.

The Leghorns have a high reputation as layers. Of these Italian fowls, the brown variety has recently become very popular. Said to have been introduced by Mr. F. J. Kinney, of Massachusetts, who bought the first trio that was imported, in 1853, from on board a ship in Boston harbor. Since then Mr. Kinney has made several importations from Leghorn, in Italy. The character of these birds is of the very best. They are yellow skinned, and excellent table fowls, are extremely hardy, and enormous layers. Hens have laid on the average 240 eggs in the year in some flocks. Pullets often begin to lay before they are five months old, and continue laying during the whole winter. They are gay plumaged birds, and have become popular amongst fanciers. The Brown Leghorns are described as having the comb of the Black Spanish fowl, with its head and body, and the plumage or color of the Black-red Game. The Brown Leghorn cock is black-breasted, with hackles of orange-red, striped with black; the ear-lobes are white. The hen is salmon-color on the breast, with the rest of the plumage brown, finely penciled with dark markings. They thrive fairly well in confinement. A prominent English poultry fancier is of the decided opinion that this breed is the best of all our "American" breeds, when size and product of eggs are taken into consideration. The Leghorns are all called in England American breeds, because American fanciers first developed them as pure breeds, and, so to speak, "brought them out."

EUROPEAN BREEDS. 161

They are non-sitters, which is a great advantage when eggs are the product mainly desired. There is scarcely any stock of the farm which is so poorly managed as the poultry, yet there is none that may be more productive.

Fig. 74.—BROWN LEGHORNS.

A yield of two or three dozen eggs and a brood of half a dozen chickens is generally considered a fair season's production for a hen. This is the consequence of keeping poor stock, or neglecting that which is better, and capable of doing better with proper treatment. Poultry may be improved by careful breeding as well as a pig or a cow. An infusion of new blood should be procured every year or two, and a bird of undoubted excellence should be bought.

THE FRENCH BREEDS—HOUDANS AND CREVECŒURS.

If profit is the chief end of poultry-keeping, and this is certainly the purpose for which farmers and those who raise poultry for the market, as well as those who compete for prizes at the poultry shows, are all in pursuit of, then the French breeds of fowls are worthy of high consideration. There is no other country in the world where poultry is so popular a product in the market, or so frequent a dish upon the tables, as in France, and a breed that is in favor there must possess positive merit. In addition to the vast number of eggs which are consumed in every possible shape in cookery, and in various arts, millions of dollars' worth are exported from France every year; and the *poulet*, variously presented, is not only a very conspicuous item on the bills of fare, but its delicacy and succulence entitle it to the prominence it enjoys. That it is acceptable in France should be to a breed a passport to popular favor everywhere. Yet the French fowls are not nearly so popular in America as they deserve to be. The Houdans and the Crevecœurs are both prolific egg-producers, grow rapidly, and possess white and juicy flesh. Yet we have admired these fowls in the yards of other people, and have listened favorably to frequent praise of their profit and their beauty. The Houdan is doubtless a very handsome and attractive bird, and a flock of them, well bred and well cared for, is very showy in the yard or the field They are square and massive about the body, with short legs, a spirited or even a fierce carriage, on account of their

Fig. 75.—GROUP OF FRENCH FOWLS.

(163)

peculiar crest, beard, and muffling, and the lively markings of their plumage, which, when perfect, is of a mixed "pebbly" black-and-white. They have the fifth toe,—a useless, objectionable member, which they inherit from the Dorking strain in their ancestry, although along with it they have the fine-flavored flesh and plump breast of that race. Their legs are gray and their bones remarkably light They are egg-producers rather than breeders; and if properly fed, the hens will lay on without stopping to "sit." They will thrive in confinement, when properly kept, as well as when roaming at large; and when allowed to range, exercise the liberty now and then with greater freedom than is convenient upon the farm. The standard of excellence of the poultry-fanciers for the Houdan is subject to some variation as to minor points, such as the shape of the comb; the fifth toe, however, is insisted upon; the feathering should be of black and white, evenly mixed, and not patchy; the saddle of the cock is tipped with straw yellow; the crest is of black and white feathers, evenly mixed, and thrown back so as to show the comb, which is double, evenly toothed upon each side, and with both sides alike in shape; the hackle is black and white, the beard and muffle almost hide the face, and the wattles are long and evenly rounded at the ends. The hen is square-bodied, and low-framed, with plumage like that of the cock; the crest is full and round and not loose and straggling or shaggy. The fifth claw is large and turned upwards, as with the cock. If good birds are procured to start with, they should breed very true to the marks; but if long closely bred, they will in time become mixed in appearance.

The Crevecœur, like the Houdan, is named from the village in France in the neighborhood of which it has long been largely bred for market. These birds are remarkably stately and handsome, although somber in color, except in the sunlight, when the golden-green reflections from the plumage make them very brilliant; but this peculiarity is only brought out in a favorable light. They are much more rarely seen than the Houdans, although as producers of eggs, and for non-sitting as well as for early maturity, and whiteness and sweetness of flesh, they surpass these. They are not winter layers, which is an objection; but when the cock is crossed upon Brahma hens, the eggs produce table birds of heavy weight, excellent quality, and in time for early marketing. They suffer nothing from confinement, and a dozen can be easily kept in a yard twenty feet square. They are very tame and friendly when petted. They excel as table birds, notwithstanding their black legs, which may be objected to by the marketmen or the cooks; this feature has no ill effect upon the color, flavor, or tenderness of the flesh, which is very white and of delicious flavor. Young birds will fatten when three months old, and have been made to weigh four pounds at that age, and at six months, with two weeks' fattening, have weighed seven pounds. The Crevecœur cock should be a heavy, compact bird, mounted upon short, thick legs; the thighs, being well feathered, tend to give the birds a heavier and more solid build. The back is broad and flat, giving a robustness to the figure, and slopes but slightly towards the tail, which is carried high. The general carriage is dignified, their sedateness being somewhat heightened by their somber coloring. The comb is two-horned or "antlered," and the crest is formed of lancet-shaped feathers, which fall backwards and do not straggle wildly in all directions, as in the Houdan The chicks are hardy when properly cared for, but early chicks of this breed are rare, on account of the late habits of the hen. The breast is full; the hackle is long and sweeps gracefully down the neck; the beard and muffle are full and low on the throat, and the plumage, as previously described, when perfect, is of a solid black, with greenish and sometimes brilliant reflections. The hen is similar in color and special points to the cock; her body is massive, and her legs strong to match her stout body. Her plumage is perfectly black, the crest is large, and the beard full, and the comb, which is horned, is much hidden in the crest.

As these birds become aged a few stray white feathers will appear in the crest, which, however, should be an objection in young birds. When but one breed is kept, the Houdan would be preferable to the Crevecœur, on account of its more lively color; but when cross-bred birds are not objected to, a few of the latter, with their remarkably beautiful color when in a bright light, their large size and handsome carriage, their desirable table qualities, and the habit of the hen to lay when others are broody, would make a very desirable addition to a flock of Brahmas or Cochins.

CHAPTER XVI.

AMERICAN BREEDS

PLYMOUTH ROCKS.

The breed known as the Plymouth Rock is generally acknowledged the best for useful purposes that has ever been bred in this country, and as especially adapted to our American climate, markets, and uses. As fowls for the farmer and raiser of market poultry, they are superior to other birds in many respects. They fill the requirements of the farm, while maintaining their purity as a breed. They are good layers, sitters, and mothers. They are excellent foragers, and, being at the same time under easy control, will bear close confinement without injury. They have the desirable characteristic of being self-reliant when roaming at will and dependent upon their own exertions, and contented and happy when restrained in close quarters.

For general purposes we know of no better fowl. They are hardy, and easily raised, and for a breed that is so large they are wonderfully active and industrious, quick and sprightly in their movements. With a good yard of Plymouth Rocks, the farmer or market-poultry raiser has a breed that fills all requirements; the farmer's object being not so much to gratify taste or a love of the beautiful and ornamental, as to keep fowls that will give a good supply of eggs through a great part of the year, and furnish in the fall and winter large-sized, compact birds, possessing a presentable color for the table.

The Plymouth Rocks were first brought to notice when the Brahmas and Cochins were leading the fashion, and did not attract particular attention; but on the score

Fig. 76.—PLYMOUTH ROCK FOWLS.

of their merits alone they have worked their way up, and earned for themselves a lasting reputation for general utility.

This breed is deservedly becoming very popular among those persons who keep fowls for profit. First among the good qualities of a fowl, is size. This the Plymouth Rocks have in an unusual degree. There are many excellent breeds of poultry which are all that can be desired except as to size, and the lack of this is fatal to their popularity; for, after all, profit is the chief object with most people in choosing a kind of fowl to keep. Hardiness of constitution and vigor, pleasing form, handsome and attractive plumage, and prolific production of eggs are all very desirable qualities in fowls, and these all belong to the breed. The future of the Plymouth Rocks will depend greatly upon the care or fortunate success with which they are bred. Difference of taste leads breeders to favor different styles, and thus "strains" are originated. If these styles are made to depart too much from a rigid standard, there is danger that an important and essential point may be sacrificed for some minor fancy. To prevent this, and to induce or enforce care and consistency in breeding, it would be well that a very close adherence to the standard be insisted upon in all exhibitions, and that a very rigid one be adopted. In the case of the birds here represented, they come fully up to the accepted standard of excellence of American breeders, and meet it in every respect. The points required are: The breast to be "broad, deep, and full," and the body to be "large, square, and compact." The form of these birds is therefore nearly perfect, and if breeders of the Plymouth Rocks vie with each other in taking advantage of favorable accidents in breeding, and in fixing them upon their strains, or in using care in selecting birds for breeding, as any skillful breeder may readily do, the future history of this breed will be a very gratifying one. Among some of seventy breeds recognized in the American standand of excellence, there are only three of American origin, viz., the old-fashioned Dominique, the Plymouth Rocks, and the Wyandottes. After some years of careful breeding the Plymouth Rock has been brought to such a condition of merit, that it is now one of the most popular breeds, and promises to be one of the most suitable for farmers and attractive to amateurs.

AMERICAN DOMINIQUES.

This old-fashioned breed is said to have been brought over by the early Puritans, and wherever bred in purity is acknowledged to be one of the best, hardiest, and most beautiful of all domestic fowls; and as there has certainly been no importation of any fowls of this breed into this country for a century, they have come to be regarded as strictly an American variety.

They are without doubt the *oldest* of the distinctive American breeds, being mentioned in the earliest poultry books as an indigenous and valued variety. In the *furore* for fancy breeds of fowls, the older sorts are sometimes wellnigh forgotten; yet it is highly probable that the American Dominiques possess as many good qualities as any of the newer breeds. If they do not reach the heavy weight of some of the latter breeds, they have great merit, and none give better satifaction to the farmer than this old American breed of Dominiques.

They should weigh from six to eight pounds when matnred.

The Dominiques are excellent layers, very hardy, unexceptionable as mothers, yet are not given to excessive incubation, and are good for the table. They grow both fat and feathers quickly, while their plain "home-spun" suits make them very suitable for countless localities where larger and more valuable-looking fowls would be liable to be stolen. The merits of this breed will recommend it to persons residing in the country as well worthy of promotion in the poultry-yard, whether as producers of eggs or of meat, or as sitters or nurses.

The color of their plumage may be described as a light steel-gray ground, with each feather distinctly striped or barred across with a darker or bluish-gray, the bars shading off gradually from dark into light. The cock is a very showy bird, with full saddle and hackle, and abundant well-curved sickle feathers. The comb should be a neat "rose" form; face, wattles, and ear-lobes should be red; wattles neat, well-rounded, and of medium size; legs bright yellow.

WYANDOTTES.

A breed which for some time was known as the "American Seabrights" has many admirers, who were instrumental in having the variety admitted to the Standard at the meeting of the American Poultry Association held at Worcester in 1883. At the same time the birds were given the name of Wyandottes.

Breeders differ in their statements of the origin of this variety, but it is generally considered to be a cross of the Brahma and Hamburg breeds. It matters little, however, what the history of the fowl is, so long as it possesses the desired characteristics. When well-bred, the Wyandottes are good layers, sitters, and mothers, and their flesh is of the finest flavor. Their plumage is white and black, each feather having a white ground and being heavily laced with black, the tail alone being solid black. They have a small rose comb, face and ear-lobes bright-red, legs free from feathers and of a rich yellow color. Hens will weigh eight to nine pounds, and cocks nine to ten pounds, when matured.

In this breed we have the rose comb like the Hamburgs, but not so large. The plumage is black-and-white-speckled, like the Hamburgs, but darker, with the black tail of the Brahma. The legs are yellow, like the Brahma, but bare like the Hamburg. Fine specimens are nearly as large as the Brahma. The effort has been

Fig. 77.—WYANDOTTE FOWLS.

in this combination to preserve the good qualities and eliminate the undesirable ones of both parent breeds. The Plymouth Rock has been a favorite with those who have wanted a plump, fat chicken of a pound and a half weight as broilers. The Wyandotte is fully its equal in this respect. It feathers with its growth, and is plump at any age, thrifty and hardy in raising, yellow-skinned, and in all respects an excellent variety for forcing early. When grown, they are plump in body and of an attractive appearance in the market. They lay a medium-sized

Fig. 78.—WYANDOTTES.

(175)

egg of dark-buff color. Their laying qualities depend much on the selections and matings of the parent stock. In markings the fowls are very handsome, the hen more so than the cock. In the main, the feathers are white with a black border, which makes them evenly and brightly speckled. The hackle is penciled white and black, and the tail black.

AMERICAN JAVAS.

In writing of our American Javas Mr. Bicknell says: They have characteristics different from any other variety; they present large size, long bodies, deep full breast, and their general make-up is just what is required for a genuine, useful superior table fowl—hardiness and beauty.

Of the two varieties, Black and Mottled, there is little difference except in plumage. They have single combs, feet are yellow, shanks free from feathers, skin yellow; when served on the table the flesh does not present that objectionable dark color common to some other breeds, but is equal to the Plymouth Rock in every particular.

CHAPTER XVII.

DISEASES OF POULTRY.

Poultry generally suffer from preventible ills. It is almost useless, and rarely ever worth while, to treat sick poultry. A chicken is hardly worth the trouble required to physic it, and nine out of ten die in spite of all the treatment that can be given them. Poultry are naturally subject to very few diseases. If kept clean, not overfed, not cooped up close, kept from foul, putrid food, supplied with clean water regularly, and have abundant pure air in their roosting-places, they live and thrive without any trouble, except in rare cases. The fatal disorders which result from ill-treatment cannot be cured by medicine. It is too late. The mischief has been done when the first symptoms appear, and the best procedure is generally to kill the diseased fowls and save the rest by sanitary measures.

DISTEMPER, ROUP, AND CHICKEN-POX.

An article which recently appeared in a poultry journal is the most practical we have ever seen on these subjects, and is well worth reprinting. Fowls never perspire; the waste of the system is in a large measure carried off in the vapor of the breath, which is far more rapid than is by many supposed. The heart of the fowl beats 150 times per minute, which causes a rapid respiration, and demands twice the amount of air in proportion to weight. Even the bones of the wing are

DISEASES OF POULTRY. 179

charged with air, and so much so that the windpipe severed and tied, and the wing sawn off, it will admit air enough to sustain life for some time.

Distemper, which seems to be an acclimated disease, yet if neglected often results in roup, is easily detected by a puffed face, deep scarlet in color, and in two or three days discharges from the nostrils appear. In this disease the membrane of the air-passages, tear-tube and throat is inflamed; and when so much so as to close the tear-tube, the discharges become acrid, and roup is the result. To prevent this, it becomes necessary to check these mucous-discharges. The use of kerosene is a handy and sure cure. By holding the fowl so it cannot swallow, and filling the throat with the oil, holding long enough to have the oil thoroughly saturate the throat, then allowing the same to run out of the mouth, and by washing the nostrils out, and injecting a few drops into each nasal passage, the effect is magical; and if attended to during the first two days of the distemper, one application generally proves sufficient. So safe and sure is this remedy that I have not used any other for the past two years. It checks at once the unnatural discharges. The breathing of kerosene for the twenty-four hours seems to have a most marvelous effect; and restoration to health is the result. By neglect we often have an attack of "roup," which is apparent in a fetid breath, swollen head, and inflamed face, a throat and mouth filled with canker. No matter what the cause that has brought this state of things to your flock,—be it bad ventilation, filthy quarters, unclean water-vessels, or neglect to remove roupy specimens till by the taint of the water by drinking in the same vessel the whole flock is effected,—it is safe, when a part of the fowls are so affected, to reason that the entire flock is in a measure poisoned in blood, and means should be taken to prevent its spreading. If we in such a case put in the water-vessel bromide of potassium to the extent of two grains to each fowl, for three or four days, the evils of the ravage may be stayed.

But in treating those bad cases described above, if the patient is so full of canker as to be unable to eat, we must administer the doses.

At the time of the Portland exhibition, I had sent to me a patient in the shape of a fine Light Brahma. The bird did not arrive until I had left for the exhibition; consequently, it was three days before I could attend to him. When I retured I found him in the following deplorable condition: His mouth was as full as it could possibly be of canker; his head was swollen till both eyes were closed, and face and comb were broken out with dry canker, or, as some poultrymen call it, chicken-pox. By the use of a large syringe, I injected the bird's crop full of milk in which four grains of bromide had been dissolved; I then gargled the mouth and throat with kerosene in the way described above.

We see many recommendations to remove the canker by forcible means; this is the very worst thing that can be done (inhuman and retards the cure). In the case of the Light Brahma, by gargling the throat three mornings, the fourth morning nearly all the canker slipped off, leaving the mouth smooth. I administered the milk and bromide for the four days also.

The head, as I have described, was a swollen, shapeless mass. I felt that the case was a hopeless one, and, already knowing the curative properties of the oil for canker in the throat, I bathed the head, face, and throat with the oil, repeating the operation the second morning, when I noticed here and there small blisters on the throat, and a decided improvement in the looks of my patient. I then on the fourth morning applied the oil again, when the swelling subsided, and he opened his eyes and commenced to eat a little, and from that time improved rapidly; the blisters of course dried down.

About a week afterward I was brushing the dry scale from face and comb, and in the process I lifted entire the cuticle and feathers from head and neck for three inches down, which demonstrated the power of the oil as a counter-irritant, and the necessity of care in its use. These two medicines are all I have used since for distemper or roup, and so successful have I been that I think it safe to say I have not lost five birds by roup in the past two years.

Chicken-pox—warty blotches of comb and throat—can be treated with bromide, by giving three grains a day, and isolating the bird till the spots dry and cleave off, which will be in a week or ten days. The plan to remove those caps is a very bad one, and only spreads the disease. Patience, giving time for the bromide to do its work, and the shedding of the dry scales, is all that is needed for a cure.

CHICKEN OR FOWL CHOLERA.

There is nothing more unsatisfactory than a sick chicken, or more difficult to treat, and we find that the best writers upon poultry diseases insist much more upon prevention than upon cures. The term "cholera" is applied to a disease which, though it varies in different parts of the country, is everywhere accompanied by a violent diarrhœa, and is rapidly fatal. In every such outbreak of disease among fowls, the first thing to be done is to separate the sick from the well, and at once give a change of food, which should be of the most nourishing character, and combined with some stimulant, such as Cayenne pepper, or a tonic, like iron. Modern writers upon poultry diseases are greatly in favor of iron in some form as a tonic. The old method of putting rusty nails in the drinking-water had good sense at the bottom of it, but a more active form of iron is desirable. The English poultrymen are much in favor of "Douglas's Mixture." This is made by putting eight ounces of sulphate of iron (also called copperas, or green vitriol) into a jug (never use a metallic vessel) with two gallons of water, and adding one ounce of sulphuric acid (oil of vitriol). This is to be put into the drinking-water in the proportion of a tea-spoonful to a pint, and is found to be a most useful tonic whenever such is needed. So soon as the disease breaks out among the poultry, this should be given to the well to enable them to resist it, together with more nutritious and easily digestible food.

One writer on the subject states that he made a saturated solution of alum, and whenever a bird was attacked, gave it two or three tea-spoonfuls, repeating the dose the next day. He mixed their feed, Indian meal, with alum-water for a week. Since adopting this he has lost no fowls. Another writes that in each day's feed of cooked Indian meal, for a dozen fowls, he added a table-spoonful of Cayenne pepper, gunpowder, and turpentine, feeding this every other day for a week. From what we have heard of chicken-cholera, it appears to be a protest against improper feeding and housing rather than any well-defined disease. Fowls are often in poor condition on account of the vermin they are obliged to support, or they may be in impaired health from continuous feeding on corn alone. When in this weakened state, a sudden change in the weather may induce diarrhea, or a cold, which attacks the flock so generally that the disease appears to be epidemic. And being generally and rapidly fatal, it is called "cholera," and the owner of such a flock at once writes us for a remedy for "chicken-cholera." A recent letter, from a friend in Massachusetts, is the type of many others received of late. This informed us that some of the fowls would leave the rest of the flock, go off and mope by themselves, refuse to eat, and, as a general thing, those so affected soon died. The writer assumed this to be cholera. Our reply was essentially as follows: Separate at once the sick birds from the well. If the poultry-house has not recently been put in order, remove all the fowls until it can be fumigated, by burning sulphur, and then whitewashed in every part of the interior with lime-wash, to each pailful of which half a pound of crude carbolic acid has been added. Mix some lard and kerosene, and, with a rag, or swab, rub all the roosts. Throw out all the old straw from the nest-boxes, and grease with the lard and kerosene the insides of these. Renew the dust-boxes, using fine road-dust, and mixing some sulphur with the dust.

SCABBY LEGS IN POULTRY.

The unsightly disease which affects the legs of fowls, causing them to swell and become distorted, is due to a mite, a small insect which is similar in appearance to that which causes scab in sheep. It is roundish-oval, and semi-transparent, about one eight-hundredth of an inch in length, appearing, when magnified 400 diameters, about half an inch long. If the scales from the leg of a diseased fowl are beneath the microscope, a number of these mites may be found between them. Beneath the scales there are spongy, scabby growths, in which the eggs and pupæ of the mites are to be seen in great numbers. The pupæ are very similar in shape to the mature mites, but are very much smaller, appearing, when viewed with the above-mentioned power, about one tenth of an inch in length. The disease, being of a similar character to the scab in sheep, or the mange in dogs and cattle, may be cured by the same treatment.

We have cured fowls of the disease, before accurately knowing the cause, by applying to the legs a mixture of lard with one-twentieth part of carbolic acid. This should be applied with a stiff brush, such as one of those sold with bottles of mucilage. A very small painter's sash-brush would answer the purpose; but something must be used by which the medicated grease can be applied thoroughly to the crevices between the scales. A mixture of equal parts of lard or sweet-oil and kerosene will be equally as effective as the carbolic-acid mixture. It is probable that lard, or oil alone, would be effective, but the kerosene more easily penetrates between the scales, and the carbolic acid is sure death to the parasites. The remedy being so simple, it will be inexcusable if this disagreeable affection is suffered to remain in a flock; while, however, one fowl is troubled with it, it will certainly spread, as the mites will burrow beneath the scales of the other fowls. If precautions were generally used, the parasite could soon be exterminated. It should be made a disqualification at poultry-shows for fowls to be affected with scabby legs or feet, in any degree whatever, for we know that several poultry-yards are not free from this disease; and whenever affected fowls are sent out, the disease goes with them.

EGG-EATING FOWLS.

When fowls are confined they will eat their eggs, and no persuasion but that of the ax will prevent them. They must be freed from confinement and given their natural employment of scratching, or they will get into this mischief.

If the bird is worth the trouble, a nest may be so arranged that the egg, when laid, will at once roll out of sight and reach.

DISEASES OF POULTRY.

FEATHER-EATING FOWLS.

The habit of pulling and eating feathers is also common among fowls confined. It is impossible to cure the fault when once acquired, and it is best to kill the fowls for table use at first sight, as they quickly teach others to do the same. The cause is doubtless a need or appetite for something contained in the feathers. A mixture of dried flesh and bone, specially prepared for poultry, with a small quantity of sulphur, will act as a preventive. Bits of fresh lean meat, or scraps, or fine-powdered fresh bones, will answer.

Another remedy is to give them a sheep's pluck, or liver, to pick at, hanging it up within reach, and to give them wheat scattered in the earth or litter of their houses. This will give them food and work to occupy their time.

THE PIP.

Poultry are sometimes troubled with a disease known as "pip." This is inflammation of the tongue and mouth, with the growth of a horny scale on the point of the tongue, which prevents the fowls from feeding. Give each fowl a pinch of powdered chlorate of potash, dropping it into the throat and upon the tongue, and remove the scale with the point of a penknife.

GAPES.

Gapes is the result of parasitic worms in the windpipe. The only cure is to dislodge them. This is sometimes successfully done by putting the chicks in a box, covering the top with a piece of muslin, and dusting fine lime through the cloth. The chicks breathe the lime, and as it comes in contact with the worms, these let go of the membranes, and are dislodged by the coughing and sneezing of the chicks. To prevent gapes, the chicks should not be kept on ground where fowls have previously been. This may be done either by spading old ground deeply each year, or providing a different locality for the poultry-yard.

EGG-BOUND FOWLS.

It is not at all uncommon for hens, especially old and infirm ones, to become egg-bound. The eggs without shells collect in the egg-passage, and form a mass of hard, cheesy matter, which in time causes the abdomen to swell, and finally kills the fowl. In the early stages of this trouble the remedy is to inject some linseed-oil into the passage, and, by dilating it with the fingers, remove the collected matter. The trouble is generally from over-feeding with stimulating food.

LOSS OF FEATHERS.

Poultry will frequently drop their feathers when over-fed upon corn, buckwheat, or other heating food. The remedy is to feed only chopped cabbage or turnips, or turn them into a grass-field for a few days. A few pills of castile-soap, or half a tea-spoonful of castor-oil, will be of benefit.

BUMBLE-FOOT.

This is usually caused by a bruise or sliver; inflammation sets in, and pus forms under the skin and be-

DISEASES OF POULTRY. 187

comes condensed into hard, cheesy matter. When discovered, while the pus is in liquid form, if the skin be opened with a knife, the pus-cavity well syringed out with carbolic acid and water, the place kept open by poulticing for a day or two, it heals up. The same trouble sometimes attacks the shank; in such a case open the sack at the bottom and top, and syringe the cavity from the top to the bottom a couple of times; then use strong liniment on the shank, and it will all heal up. When the case is of so long standing that the pus becomes hard and cheesy, the only way is to lay the whole thing open, making an opening large enough to press the core out; then poultice and use the carbolic acid and water baths, finally winding up with a strong liniment.

DEFENSE AGAINST DISEASE.

If cared for, and they have clean, wholesome quarters and not crowded, poultry will always be healthy. If a fowl merely acts a little "cranky," do not imagine that it is sick, and commence stuffing it with drugs; simply remove it to a pen some distance from the flock, and let it alone a few days. If it proves to be very sick, chop off its head and burn it. For cholera, a strong solution of hyposulphite of soda, given three times a day, in teaspoonful doses, is probably the best remedy we have. For gapes, dip a feather in turpentine, and insert it into the windpipe. One application will generally cure; two are sometimes necessary. Dip scaly legs in kerosene two or three times. A little sulphur mixed with the food once a week in winter prevents packing of the crop and irregularities of the bowels, caused by overeating and the constant production of eggs. Gravel and coarse sand are necessary for the digestion of food. Crushed bones, old plaster, lime, etc., are necessary for the formation of egg-shells. Cayenne pepper in small quantities, mixed with the food occasionally during the winter, promotes egg-laying.

CHAPTER XVIII.

PARASITES UPON POULTRY.

It is very common to speak of "Hen-lice" as if there were but one kind of insect parasite upon our fowls. The fact is that there are at least five species of lice which, with several mites, ticks, and kindred creatures, bring up the number of poultry pests to a dozen or more. From the day the chick leaves the egg, to that on which it is prepared for market, it is subject to the attacks of one or more of these parasites. That they interfere with the comfort, and consequently the thrift of the birds, is evident, and to be a successful poultry-raiser one should know thoroughly the habits of these poultry enemies and the methods of getting rid of them. That some are wonderfully prolific is shown by feathers sent us by a friend in New Hampshire, who writes: "They have something on the base, and about every feather in the 'fluff' is like these." (See Fig. 79.) The engraving, of the natural size, gives the appearance of the feathers. A magnifier showed the "something on the base" to be a dense mass of the eggs of a parasite, and it is safe to say that there were several hundreds in each cluster. A portion of the eggs had hatched, and we do not wonder that our friend wrote that the "cockerel is very lousy." Some of the creatures live only upon the feathers of the

Fig. 79.—EGGS AT BASE OF FEATHER.

bird, while others are provided with suckers by which to draw the blood. Where the fowls are in good health, and have free use of the dust bath, they keep the parasites from excessive increase. In winter there should always be a box of fine earth for dusting kept where no water can reach it. Old nest-boxes should be treated to a bath of scalding lye before they are again used.

To get rid of fleas, the chicken-house should be thoroughly whitewashed—not half done—with hot lime-wash. The floor should be well sprinkled with a solution of carbolic acid, and the roosts thoroughly greased with a mixture of one pound of lard, one pint of raw linseed oil, a quarter of a pint of kerosene, and a quarter of a pound of sulphur.

When kerosene oil is placed on the fowls themselves, it should be used sparingly; properly applied, it is the best known remedy for lice, but to use it recklessly is dangerous.

"THE" HEN LOUSE.

Unfortunately for the fowls, it is impossible to describe "*the*" Hen Louse, for there are so many of them. Here is a portrait, Fig. 80, of one of the easiest to find, as it is one of the largest, being nearly $\frac{1}{12}$ inch long. Unless special care is taken, little chicks, when they are first hatched, are sadly afflicted; and the feathers on the head are all alive with them. Not only common fowls, but all other domestic birds, including the delicate pets, such as the canary, and the wild birds from the largest to the smallest, are infested by *parasites* —as animals and plants that live upon other animals and plants are called. Vermin is the pest of poultry, and when chicken-houses get thoroughly infested, it is not an easy matter to cleanse them. If the house is washed with a hot-lime wash, and the roosts are rubbed with a mixture of kerosene oil and lard, the lice will be made uncomfortable, and if this treatment is repeated a few times, the house and also the fowls will be quite free from vermin. If the house is, as all poultry houses should be, detached from barns and other buildings, it may be fumigated. Shut it up tight and close every opening; then place a pan of live coals on the ground (or if it must be on a wooden floor, put down a few shovelfuls of earth, or cold ashes to hold the pan). Throw on a handful of lumps of brimstone, and get out quickly, closing the door tightly. If the work has been done thoroughly, no lice can be found at the end of a few hours. The white-washing, etc., may then be done.

In regard to the use of kerosene, it is not more effective perhaps than some other remedies, but is applied more easily than lard, tobacco, sulphur, or whitewash. We apply it to the perches in the hennery from the common lamp-filler. Turn a very small stream from the spout, and move the can rapidly from end to end of the perch.

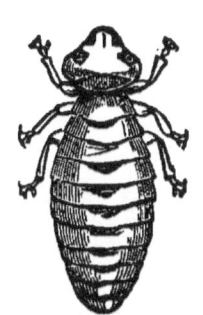

Fig. 80.—LARGE PALE HEN-LOUSE.

The oil gets upon the feet and feathers, and is soon distributed all over the fowl. The lice leave on very short notice, and the fowls are entirely relieved. It is a greater safeguard against lice on chickens, when first hatched, to use the oil in the boxes, before the nest is made for the sitting hen. It takes but a small quantity, applied to the corners of the box, to keep away insects. Take care that the oil does not touch the eggs. In using a substance like kerosene about the farm buildings, remember that it is inflammable, and must be employed with caution, avoiding every chance of fire.

While the kerosene will destroy vermin by the thou-

192 PROFITS IN POULTRY.

sands, its effects are not lasting, as it soon evaporates. To be effectual, it should be applied to the roosts and wood-work frequently, say once a week.

The red color of some of the lice is due to the blood sucked by them from the fowls, as mosquitoes become red after dining on human blood.

CHAPTER XIX.

RAISING TURKEYS.

It is a joyful morning to the farmer when he discovers his first brood of young turkeys following the cautious tread and the low cluck of the mother, as she leaves her nest. The critical season of turkey-raising is now before him. Upon his constant care and watchfulness for the next three or four weeks depend his success and his profits. It is a matter of the first importance that the care of the young broods should be committed to some one individual. There is no substitute for personal responsibility in carrying the young chicks through their first month. They are very tender, and they have many enemies from the start. The mother bird has wise instincts to guard her brood against harm in a state of nature, but in domestication she needs close watching to guard them against birds and beasts of prey, against roaming for food too early in the morning, and especially against storms. If the farmer cannot attend to this himself, he should put the care upon some one else who will look after the broods at short intervals during the day, and see them properly sheltered for the night. Women who have a fondness for the work make the best guardians of the young broods. Each little flock should be counted every night, as they come to their roost, and if any are missing they should be looked after. They can be controlled in their wanderings, at first, by frequent feeding. Like all other birds, they follow the feed very strictly, and will not wander very far from food that is regularly and bountifully supplied.

Why is it that one farmer will raise nearly every turkey-chick that comes out of the shell, and do this nine years out of ten, without much respect to wet or dry seasons, while another loses from a half to three quarters with about the same uniformity? We know of men with whom success is the established rule. They are very systematic in this, as in all their other business. We visited one of these thrifty farmers, who raised one hundred and sixty-five turkeys last year from nine hens, and upon inquiry found that he did about the same thing every year. We wanted to know just how he managed

Fig. 81.—BRONZE TURKEY.

to secure this uniform result, and found him communicative. He insists upon good stock to begin with—the best always selected to breed from. Then he places great reliance upon regular feeding during the fall and winter, so that the flock becomes very gentle, and the hens make their nests immediately about the sheds and barns in places prepared for them. This is a great safeguard against foxes, skunks, crows, hawks, and other creatures that destroy the birds or their eggs. When the young first come off the nest, they are confined in pens for a few days until they are strong enough to fly over a board inclosure one foot high. He feeds frequently with coarse corn-meal and sour milk until four o'clock in the afternoon. He found in his experience that he lost a good many chicks from the food hardening in the crop. There is danger from over-feeding. As the chicks grow the sour-milk diet is increased, and during the summer it is kept constantly in a trough for them. They are exceedingly fond of sour-milk and buttermilk, and they grow very rapidly upon this diet. An incidental advantage, and a very important one, he thinks, is that the young birds are prevented from straying very far from the house. They return many times during the day to the buttermilk trough for their favorite food. This, with Indian meal, constitutes their principal food until midsummer, when insects are more abundant, and they wander farther from the house. This method can easily be tried on dairy farms.

TURKEY ROOSTS.

The turkey instinctively goes to roost at nightfall, and in its native haunts takes to the highest trees, in order to be safe from numerous enemies. The domesticated bird has the same instinct, and prefers the roofs of buildings, or the branches of trees, to any perch under cover. Yet, if taken in hand when the broods are young, turkeys can be trained to roost in almost any place not under cover. For safety the roost should be near the house or barn. If left to roost upon fences or trees at a distance from the house, they are liable to be disturbed, or carried off by foxes, or by poultry-thieves. The roost should be some fifteen or twenty feet from the ground. Poles of red or white cedar, from three to five inches in diameter, are the best material, and these are the most convenient sizes for the scaffolding upon which the birds are to roost. The odor of these woods is a protection against the vermin which sometimes infest the young birds. The size of the poles for the roosts is a matter of importance. It is much easier for these heavy birds to keep their balance upon a large pole than upon a small one. Then, in the freezing weather of winter, the feet of the birds are more completely protected by the feathers. Another advantage of having the turkeys roost together is the saving of manure. If the ground under the roost is kept covered with muck, or loam, and occasionally stirred, several loads of a valuable fertilizer may be made every season. A roost made of durable wood, like cedar, will last for a lifetime. It is but a little trouble to train the young broods to go to their roost every night. And after the habit has once been formed they will go to the same roosting-place regularly every night. One of the secrets of success in turkey-raising is in having a secure roosting-place.

FATTENING TURKEYS.

It is a goodly sight, as the summer days wane, to see the flocks of turkeys coming home from the woods and pastures at nightfall with full crops. If the farm has not been overstocked with these birds, they have very largely made their living upon grasshoppers, crickets, worms, and other small fry. The regular food they have had has been rather to keep them wonted than to supply any lack of forage. As the cool nights come on, and the supply of insects declines, the business of fattening properly commences. It should be remembered that plump, well-dressed turkeys not only bring a higher price in market, but enhance the reputation of the producer, and make his market sure for future years. The turkey is one of the finished products of the farm and one of the greatest luxuries in the market. The farmer should do his best in preparing his flock for the shambles. The main business now is to lay on fat, and the bird should have, every night and morning, a full supply of nutritious and fattening food. Instinctively the turkey follows his feed, and if the supply is abundant at the farm-yard he will not stroll far from home. Boiled potatoes, mashed, and mixed with meal, and fed moderately warm, is a very excellent feed both to promote growth and to fatten. If the pigs can be robbed of a part of their milk, and it be mixed with a part of the hot potatoes and meal, it will very much improve the dish. It is very desirable to supply the place of insects with some kind of animal food, and butchers' scraps is one of the cheapest and most desirable forms of food for poultry. Grain should be given at least once a day with the soft and warm feed. Nothing is better than sound corn. The Northern corn is thought to contain more oil than that of Southern growth. Old corn should always be used for this purpose. The new corn keeps them too loose. In feeding, only so much corn should be thrown out as the birds will eat up clean. Take a little time to feed them, and study æsthetics as you watch the iridescent hues upon the glossy plumage. There is nothing more charming upon the farm in the whole circle of our feathered dependants than a hundred or two of these richly bronzed turkeys feeding near the corn-crib. You can afford to enjoy the disappearance of corn, while the turkeys are increasing in weight. Dreams of a full wallet at Thanksgiving and Christmas will not harm you as you look on this interesting sight.

HABITS OF THE WILD TURKEY.

The males commence wooing as early as February in some of the extreme Southern States; but March is the opening of the season throughout the country, and April the month in which it reaches its highest development. The males may then be heard calling to the females from every direction, until the woods ring with their loud and liquid cries, which are commenced long ere the sun appears above the horizon, and continued for hours with the steadiest persistency. As both sexes roost apart at this period, the hens avoid answering the gobblers for some time, but they finally become less obdurate, and coyly return the call. When the males hear this, all within hearing respond promptly and vehemently, uttering notes similar to those which the domestic gobblers do when they hear an unusual sound. If the female answering the call is on the ground, the males fly to her and parade before her with all the pompous strutting that characterizes the family. They spread and erect their tails, depress their wings with a quivering motion and trail them along the ground, and draw the head back on the shoulders, as if to increase their dignity and importance; then wheel, and march, and swell, and gobble, as if they were trying to outdo each other in airs and graces. The female, however, pays little attention to these ceremonious parades, and demurely looks on while the rivals for her affection try to outdo one another in playing the gallant and dandy. When the strutting and gobbling fail to win her, the candidates for matrimony challenge each other to mortal combat, and whichever is successful in the contest walks away with her in the most nonchalant manner. The easy indifference of the hen as to which she will follow may not be pleasing to persons imbued with romantic feelings, yet she is only obeying a wise

Fig. 82.—WILD TURKEY COCK.

law of nature, which decrees that only the fittest should live, and in the lower animal world these are necessarily chosen for their physical qualities.

The battles between the males are often waged with such desperate valor that more than one combatant is sent to join the great majority, as they deliver very heavy blows at each other's heads, and do not give up a contest until they are dead, or so thoroughly exhausted as to be scarcely able to move.

When one has killed another, he is said sometimes to caress the dead bird in an apparently affectionate manner, as if it were very sorry to have been compelled to do such a deed, but could not help it, owing to the force of circumstances; yet I have seen the winner in a tournament in such a rage that it not only killed its rival, but pecked out its eyes after it was dead. When the victors have won their brides, they keep together until the latter commence laying, and then separate, for the males would destroy the eggs if they could, and the hens, knowing this, carefully screen them. The males are often followed by more than one hen; but they are not so polygamous as their domestic congeners, as I never heard of a gobbler having more than two or three females under his protection. The adult gobblers drive the young males away during the erotic season, and will not even permit them to gobble if they can help it; so that the latter are obliged to keep by themselves, generally in parties of from six to ten, unless some of the veterans are killed, and then they occupy the vacated places, according to the order of their prowess.

Some aged males may also be found wandering through the woods in parties of two, three, four or five, but they seldom mingle with the flocks, owing, apparently, to approaching old age. They are exceedingly shy and vigilant, and so wild that they fly immediately from an imaginary danger created by their own suspicious nature. They strut and gobble occasionally, but not near so much as their younger kindred. Barren hens, which also keep by themselves, are almost as demonstrative in displaying their vocal powers, airs, and feathers as the old males, whereas they are exceedingly coy and unpretentious when fertile. When the season is over, the males keep by themselves in small bachelor parties; but, instead of being exceedingly noisy as they were in the early part of the mating period, they become almost silent. Yet they sometimes strut and gobble on their roosts, though, as a general rule, they do not, and content themselves with elevating and lowering the tail feathers and uttering a puffing sound. They keep at this exercise for hours at a time on moonlight nights without rising from their perch, and sometimes continue it until daylight.

When the hen is ready to lay, she scratches out a slight hollow in a thicket, a cane brake, beside a prostrate tree, in tall grass or weeds, or in a grain field, and lines it rudely with grass or leaves, and then deposits her eggs in it. These, which vary in number from ten to twenty, are smaller and more elongated than those of the domestic turkey, and are of a dull cream or a dirty white color, sprinkled with brownish-red spots. Audubon says that several hens may lay their eggs in one nest, and hatch them and raise the broods together. He found three hens sitting on forty-two eggs in a single nest, and one was always present to protect them.

If the eggs are not destroyed, only one brood is raised in a year; but if they are, the female calls loudly for a male, and when she is rejoined by one, both keep company until she is ready to commence laying again, when she deserts him or drives him away. She builds her nest in the most secluded spot she can find, and covers it carefully with leaves or grass whenever she leaves it.

GENERAL HINTS ABOUT TURKEYS.

The greatly increased attention paid to the turkey crop in the Eastern States, and in the Southern and Western States as well, seems to call for a few more notes. Without a good range it will not pay to raise turkeys; they create trouble between neighbors. I have found that, when confined to a yard, one turkey will require as much food to bring it to maturity as will make forty pounds of pork on a well-bred pig. Where they can have extensive range, they will pick up most of the food they require until autumn. The young are very delicate, and the hen must be cooped until they are well feathered and able to look out for themselves. The same food recommended for chicks is suitable for turkeys. Two weeks before marketing, confine them in a small, clean pen, and feed them all they will eat, not forgetting plenty of fresh water and gravel, and they will fatten up quickly and nicely.

TURKEY-NESTS.

In the wild state the hen seeks the most secluded and inaccessible spot, where there is protection from birds and beasts of prey. Security against attack is the main thing that instinct prompts her to look out for. A tangled thicket of briers, a sheltering ledge, a hollow stump, a clump of brush filled with decaying leaves, suit her fancy. With little preparation she drops her eggs upon the bare ground in these secluded places. Domesticated turkeys usually are left to a good deal of freedom in choosing their nests. Some farmers have prepared nests, made of loose stones and boards, or old barrels, placed by the roadside, or near the barn, and slightly covered with old brush. These are often exposed to the attack of weasles and skunks, and other enemies, besides being unsightly. If there are no prepared nests they will seek the nearest bit of woods, or patch of brush, or fence-corner, where they can find shelter. The whole turkey crop for the year is put in jeopardy by this want of preparation for the laying and breeding season. By having a yard devoted to fruit trees and turkeys, and an open shed with sliding doors, you have complete control of the birds, their eggs and their young, during their tender age. The risk is reduced to a minimum, and the turkey crop is as sure as any other raised on the farm. The nests under the shed should be about three feet square, and arranged with slats in the front so that the birds may be shut in or out at pleasure. The common A-shaped hen-coop on a larger scale, the peak of the gable being about three feet high, is a very good arrangement. If the turkeys are fed under the shed for a few weeks before the laying season, they will take kindly to the nests prepared for them.

EARLY BROODS.

Early broods are very desirable on several accounts, but there is a good deal of risk in having the chicks come out before the grass is well started, and there is settled weather. In the latitude of 40°, and northward, it is quite early enough to have the chicks out by the middle of May. Birds hatched from the middle of May until July 1st will have five or six months in which to grow before Thanksgiving, and that is as soon as they will be wanted for slaughter or to sell as stock. The cold storms of April and early May are likely to prove fatal to the chicks. The laying of the hens is very much within the control of their owner, and can be hastened or retarded by more or less feed at his pleasure. Some of our best breeders feed light after the first of February for the purpose of delaying the laying season. They do not care to have chicks before the first of June. Coming out at that date, they feel reasonably sure of raising the large majority of the hatch. After the birds have begun to lay, and get used to the nests, it is well to feed generously to keep up the strengh of the hen while she is laying, and so prepare her for the sitting season. The number of eggs that a hen will lay depends a good deal upon the feed. The average is from fifteen to thirty eggs, while in some cases among the thoroughbreds they keep on laying all summer without manifesting any desire to sit upon the nest. These perpetual layers become very much exhausted in the fall, and it takes them a long time to recover.

SETTING THE HEN-TURKEYS.

As turkeys require a good deal of attention while they are upon their nests, they should be in one yard, or building, or at least not far distant from one another, to take up as little time as possible in the frequent visits. In making the nests, study nature and build upon the bare earth, lined with leaves or hay, or any convenient soft substance; give the eggs room enough, and yet have the nest deep enough to prevent their rolling out of the nest. A hen will lay from fifteen to thirty eggs at a litter, but they cannot always cover the whole litter. Very large old birds will cover twenty eggs. Smaller birds will cover from fifteen to eighteen, and this is about the right average. If you have a dozen turkey-hens in your flock, which is about the right number for a good range, it will not be difficult to set several birds at once, and these may be arranged in nests within a few feet of each other. With artificial or addled eggs you can keep a part of the hens upon their nests a few days, until three or four are ready. Then select eggs of as near equal age as possible and put them under the hens. If the hens, close together, are not set at the same time, there is danger when the first begins to hatch that her neighbors will hear the peep of the first chicks, and become uneasy, and perhaps forsake their nests. If all in the group of three or four nests are hatching at the same time, there is no trouble of this kind. Before putting the eggs into the nest, it is well to sprinkle a little snuff among the hay to guard against insects. If any of the eggs get fouled with the yolk of a broken egg before or after setting, the shells should be carefully cleaned with tepid water, to secure their hatching. Two or three turkeys will sometimes lay in the same nest. This will not do any harm in the early part of the season, but they should be separated before setting, and only one bird allowed to the nest. This may be done by making nests near by and putting a porcelain or addled egg in each new nest. Turkeys are not apt to crowd on to an occupied nest when a vacant one is close by. The group of hens that sit together, and bring off their young at the same time, will naturally feed and ramble together, and this will save a good deal of time in looking after them. The turkey is a close sitter, and will not leave her nest for several days at a time. Grain and water should be kept near the nests.

FEEDING AND RAISING THE CHICKS.

One of the secrets of successful poultry-raising is the art of feeding properly, not merely at regular intervals, but on the most suitable food, and keeping the chicks growing as rapidly as possible from the very start. It is very poor economy to stint turkeys, especially young growing stock; for when once stunted, it takes a long while to recover, if it does occur at all. For the first twenty-four hours after the chicks emerge from the shell, they should remain under the hen unmolested, both to dry and gain strength and hardiness. They do not require any food, as the store nature provides will last over this time. As the chicks hatch sometimes irregularly, the older ones can be cared for in the house until the others are ready to be taken away, when the hen and her brood can be removed to a roomy coop, with a tight-board bottom and a rain-proof roof. They should be fed five times daily, but only just what they will eat up clean. The first food should consist of stale bread moistened in water or in fresh milk—the milk is decidedly preferable. Do not wet the food, as very moist or sloppy food will cause sickness and a high rate of mortality among young, tender birds. If milk can be spared, give it to them freely in place of water.

The too lavish use of corn-meal has caused more deaths among young chicks than has cholera among grown fowls. Until the chicks are half-grown, corn-meal should be but sparingly fed; but after that time, when judiciously used, is one of the very best and cheapest foods for fowls and chicks. Nine-tenths of the young turkeys and guinea-fowls which die when in the "downy" state get their death-blow from corn-meal, as it is a very common practice (because it is so "handy" and suits lazy people so well) to merely moisten with cold water some raw corn-meal and then feed it in that way.

Young chicks relish occasional feeds of cracked wheat and wheat screenings; while rice, well boiled, is not only greedily eaten by the chicks, but is one of the very best things that can be given. It frequently happens that damaged lots of rice, or low grades of it, can be bought at low figures in the cities. As it increases so much in bulk in cooking, it is not an expensive food for young chicks, even at the regular retail price, though it would not ordinarily pay to feed it to full-grown fowls very liberally or very frequently. In the absence of worms, bugs, etc., during early spring, cheap parts of fresh beef can be well boiled and shredded up for the little chicks; but care must be taken not to feed more frequently than once in two days, and only then in moderation. This feeding on meat shreds is very beneficial to young turkeys and guinea chicks when they are " shooting" their first quill feathers, as then they require extra nourishment to repair the drain on immature and weakly bodies.

LOSS OF WEIGHT IN DRESSING TURKEYS.

Farmers frequently have occasion to sell turkeys by live weight, and wish to know what is the fair relative price between live and dead weight. In turkeys dressed for the New York market, where the blood and feathers only are removed, the loss is very small. For the Eastern markets the head is cut off and the entrails are taken out. This makes a loss of nearly one tenth in the weight. A large gobbler was recently killed weighing alive $31\frac{1}{2}$ lbs. After bleeding and picking he weighed $29\frac{1}{2}$ lbs., a loss of 2 lbs., or about one-fifteenth. When ready for the spit he weighed $28\frac{1}{4}$ lbs.—a loss of $3\frac{1}{4}$ lbs., which is very nearly one-tenth of the weight. Where the market requires the New York style of dressing, and the price is 15 cents a pound, a farmer could afford to sell at 14 cents live weight, or less, if he counted the labor of dressing anything. In the other style of dressing, if the price were 20 cents, he could sell for 18 cents, or less, live weight, without loss. Farmers who have never tested the loss of weight in dressing sometimes submit to a deduction of three or four cents a pound from the middlemen, who are interested in making this large difference. We have no means of knowing the exact cost of dressing turkeys, but half a cent a pound would probably be a large estimate. The prevailing higher price of dressed turkeys in the Eastern market is not owing simply to the difference in the style of dressing, though this has something to do with it. A large portion of the turkeys that go to the Boston and Providence markets are of extra large size, principally of the Bronze and Narragansett breeds and their crosses, raised in Rhode Island and Eastern Connecticut, where the farmers make it a specialty. Whole flocks of young birds will dress about 12 lbs., on the average, at Thanksgiving, and 14 lbs. or more at Christmas. Young cocks frequently reach 18 to 20 lbs. dressed during the winter, and adult cocks 28 to 30 lbs. These birds are prepared for the market in the nicest style, and are shipped by the ton for the holidays. They always bring extra prices.

CHAPTER XX.

RAISING GEESE.

With suitable facilities, breeding geese is profitable, and many a farmer's wife has secured home comforts from this source. It is useless to breed geese with too little room; they must have their liberty to do well, and be furnished with large grass runs, as they are great graziers. Their weakness for fruit, and their ability to trample down small fruits and vegetables, make them undesirable where there are fruit and vegetable plantations. They must be kept away from young chicks, or they will soon destroy them, especially during the hatching season, when they are unusually cross and combative.

Choose only those free from all defects, either individual or hereditary. It is the rule with good breeders to keep the same birds for years successively for breeding, as the progeny is usually stronger and healthier from such stock than from younger ones. The ganders, however, rapidly depreciate with age, and also early pair off with single females. In these cases, a young and vigorous gander is substituted. It is best to make the selection for breeding in autumn, just before culling out for fattening, or selling stock to others. No amount of persuasion, or tempting high price, should induce the breeder to part with his best birds; for if he desires to steadily improve his flock, no matter whether it is of so-called common birds or thoroughbreds, he must take his pick first of the very cream of the flock.

If geese can be set early, two broods may be obtained from each female, thus securing large flocks for each season's sales. The later-hatched birds, generally having favorable weather, will make good weights by late fall, especially if given extra care and food. These late birds make excellent eating about Christmas-time. The goose usually makes her own nest, though it is well to help

Fig. 83.—PAIR OF TOULOUSE.

her a little. She is a careful and constant mother, but her love for the water must be restrained until the goslings are a few weeks old, for many dangers, in the form of musk-rats, snakes, turtles, etc., lurk at the water's edge.

Goslings do not require much extra feed, if they can get all the fresh and tender grass they want, and unless this can be supplied, breeding geese is not profitable. For the first few weeks some food must be given; this should never be corn-meal, for nine-tenths of the mortality among fledgelings, of the various kinds of domestic fowls, can readily be traced to feeding corn-meal. Cottage cheese, or dry curds of sour milk in which red pepper (Cayenne) has been sprinkled, is a very good food, and a quantity of fresh onion-tops, chopped up fine, is relished by them. Stale bread soaked in fresh milk makes an excellent food for all young birds, and the way they develop when fed liberally with it will astonish any one who has not before tried it with his fowls. The greater part of the management of geese consists in keeping them (the goslings) free from dampness while they are still "downy," guarding them from the attacks of rats, cats, weasels, and other of their enemies, in housing them well at night, and in giving them a fresh grass run as often as possible. When they become fully feathered, they are abundantly able to take care of themselves; many breeders then let the geese find their own food, which they can readily do on a large farm, until fattening time, or when the grass begins to get short, when they are brought up, and liberally and regularly fed with corn, still being permitted to have their liberty, until a week or two before they are to be killed, when they are penned up and fed with all they can eat.

VARIETIES.

In breeding for mere fancy, no doubt the odd or handsome kinds, like the white or the brown China, etc., would be satisfactory; but where heavy weights, hardi-

Fig. 84.—TOULOUSE GOOSE.

(213)

ness, and prolificness are concerned, the Toulouse and Embden are superior to all other sorts, and mature early. The common gray goose possesses the markings of its parent, the wild goose of Europe and Asia, known in England as the "Gray Lag." The fine variety known as the Toulouse has the same colors, except that the dark plumage is of much richer hues, and, by contrast at least, the light feathers whiter, while the bill and legs are of a deep orange color. The Toulouse geese early develop a deep-hanging fold of skin, pendent, like the keel of a boat, beneath the body. The evidence that the breed originated in the vicinity of Toulouse, in France, is meagre. Nevertheless, we cannot countenance the suggestion that they received their name because their skin was *too loose* for them. The first of the variety which were seen in England came, it is said, from Marseilles, in the south of France. Those purchased probably came from Toulouse to Marseilles, for this name is applied to no distinct variety in France.

Toulouse geese, when not inordinately forced for exhibition, are hardy, early layers, and reasonably prolific, often raising two broods of goslings a year. The young early take care of themselves on good pasture, and grow with astonishing rapidity. It is not well to let them depend wholly upon grass, but at first to give a little wet-up oatmeal daily, and afterwards a few oats or handfuls of barley, thrown into a trough or shallow pool to which they have access. These fine fowls attain, on a good grass range, nearly double the weight of common geese, and, forced by high feeding, a pair have been known to reach the weight of sixty pounds. Twenty-pound geese are not rare. Early goslings, if well fed, will attain that weight at Christmas. The fact is, that common geese make a poor show upon the table unless they are very fat. This is distasteful to many persons, and they can hardly be very fat before the late autumn, because we need grain to fatten them. With this variety, however, and the Embden, which matures early and attains a great weight also, it is different; the goslings are heavy before they are fat, carry a good deal of flesh, and are tender and delicious early in the season, when simply grass-fed, or having had but little grain.

Fig. 85.—PAIR OF EMBDEN GEESE.

In breeding geese, the surplus stock of goslings is killed off every year. None need be saved for wintering and breeding, except it may be well to keep one or two fine geese to take the places of old birds killed or hurt by some accident. Geese lay regularly, brood and rear their goslings well for fifty to eighty years, and it is said grow tougher every year. So if one has a good breeding goose, one which does her own duty well, and is reasonably peaceable towards other inhabitants of the farm-yard, it is best to keep her for years. Sometimes a goose will be very cross, killing ducklings and chickens, attacking children, etc. Such a one is a fit candidate for the spit.

Ganders are generally much worse, and usually one more than five or six years old becomes absolutely unbearable. So provision is naturally made to replace the old ganders every three or four years. It is, besides necessary to do so, for, though a young gander will attend four geese very well, an old one confines his attentions to one only, and often proves infertile at six or eight years old, getting crosser all the time.

PLUCKING.

A part of the profit of keeping geese depends upon their yield of feathers. When geese are bred carefully for exhibition and sale at high prices, only old ones should be plucked, and they only once or twice in the season. But when raised for market, the old ones may be plucked three times, and the young ones once before killing time, and the flock ought to yield, on an average, 18 to 20 ounces of dry feathers, besides considerable down at the summer pickings.

Common geese will yield about a pound of feathers a year, if close picked, and they are often picked cruelly close. This is unnecessary, for at the right time the feathers have a very slight hold, and the operation of plucking them is painless.

CHAPTER XXI.

RAISING DUCKS.

PROFITS IN DUCK RAISING.

Most farmers have a prejudice against water-fowl, especially ducks. They tolerate geese better than ducks, because they will forage for themselves, and live wholly on grass through the summer, after the goslings are started. Ducks will not bear neglect so well; they are more prone to wander and get lost or devoured in swamps or brooks. They have a foolish way of dropping their eggs in water, and of following a brook, or river, into neighboring farms; unless they have suitable quarters, and receive regular attention, it is a good deal of trouble to look after them. The half-starved duck disposes of a good deal of corn at a single feed, remembering the past and anticipating the future. The slipshod farmer is prejudiced against the bird, and will have none of him. But the duck has so many good qualities, matures so early, and furnishes so rare a repast, that the owner of a country home with cultivated tastes can hardly afford to do without a duck-yard. The flesh, in our esteem, is the greatest delicacy raised upon the farm; and if they were much more troublesome than we have ever found them, we should not hesitate to keep them. The fact is, a large part of the trouble is owing to sheer neglect, and the reputation of the bird as a gross feeder is owing to irregular supplies of food. If grain or other food is kept within reach, they devour no more than other fowls that mature as rapidly. If in suitable quarters and well fed, they get most of their growth in four months, and can be marketed in August at the watering-places when prices are highest. The impression that a pond or brook is necessary to raise the ducklings is erroneous. They need no more water than chickens until they are three months old, and are better off without any pond to swim in. We have raised fifty in a season in a quarter-acre yard, and found them no more troublesome than chickens. The best mothers are hens, and we prefer the Asiatic fowls, either Cochins or Brahmas. A hen of these breeds will cover nine or ten eggs. We have found an old barrel with a board at the end to fasten the bird upon her nest, as good as a more expensive coop. They are let off regularly at noon every day, when they have a half hour's range green food, grain and water. The young ducks are fed with some fresh animal food and coarse Indian meal scalded; this, varied with chopped cabbage, turnips, worms, and liver, is the staple food until they are three months old. They do much better on soft food than on grain.

The paradise of ducks is a location on a tide-water stream or cove, where there is a constant succession of sea-food with every tide. If furnished with a little house or pen upon the shore, and a variety of grain, they will come home regularly every night and lead an orderly life. The eggs are usually laid at night, or early in the morning, and very few of them need be lost. Of the four varieties, Rouen, Aylesbury, Cayuga, and Pekin, we give the preference to the last for size, early maturity, abundance of eggs, hardiness, and domestic habits.

A plan of a convenient house is shown by the accompanying engraving. For fifty to one hundred ducks it should be thirty feet long, twelve feet wide, and from four feet high at the front to six or eight feet in the rear. Entrance doors are made in the front, which should have a few small windows. At the rear are the nests; these are boxes open at the front. Behind each nest is a small door through which the eggs may be taken. It is necessary to keep the ducks shut up in the morning until they have laid their eggs, and a strip of wire netting will be required to inclose a narrow yard in front of the house. Twine netting should not be used, as the ducks put their heads through the meshes and twist the twine about their necks, often so effectively

Fig. 86.—DUCK HOUSE.

as to strangle themselves. To avoid all danger, the wire fence should have a three or four-inch mesh.

Among the most profitable varieties as layers are the Pekins. A fair yearly product for a duck in its second year is a hundred and twenty eggs, and sixty to eighty for a yearling. Their feathers are of the best quality, white, with a creamy shade; and five ducks weighing five pounds each have yielded, killed in the winter-time when fully feathered, more than one pound in all. It will be right to pick the ducks when moulting is begin-

Fig. 87.—PAIR OF PEKIN DUCKS.

(221)

ning; the feathers are then loose and are picked easily and without injury. This will considerably increase the yield of feathers, and will prevent a useless loss; otherwise the loose feathers from twenty ducks will be found spread over their whole range.

It by no means follows because ducks are a water-fowl that much water is required to raise them. Yet this is a very common impression, and multitudes of farmers and villagers deny themselves the enjoyment and profit of a flock of ducks because they have no pond or stream near the house. It is true that adult ducks will get a good deal of their living out of a water privilege, if they have one. It is not true that water to swim in is essential to their profitable keeping. They want some range and grass and good fresh water to drink every day. Ordinarily, ducks can be profitably raised wherever hens can be. They make a pleasing variety in the poultry-yard, and all who have room for them can enjoy them. The first thing in raising ducks is to get them out of the shell, and for incubation we decidedly prefer hens to ducks. They sit more steadily, and take much better care of the young. The wetting of the ducks' eggs daily in the last two weeks of incubation is even more necessary than for hens' eggs. This is sometimes done by sprinkling water upon them, but we think it better to take them from the nest and put them in a basin of tepid water about blood-warm. This moistens the whole shell without chilling the embryo life within. The ducklings out of the shell may be allowed to remain upon the nest with the hen for a day. The hen may then be put upon a grass-plat, under a coop, where the ducklings can go in and out at pleasure. Or if the hen is allowed liberty, the ducklings should be confined in a small pen from which they cannot escape. A dozen in a pen ten feet square is enough for the first two weeks. For water they only want a shallow pan—so shallow that they cannot swim, and in which they can wade at pleasure. The water should be changed often and kept in good drinking condition. For the first food nothing is better than the yolk of hard-boiled eggs or boiled liver, chopped very fine. The food had better all be cooked for the first week. It may then gradually be changed to coarse scalded Indian meal, oatmeal, wheaten grits, or rice, as suits the convenience of the feeder. Bread-crumbs and sour milk are excellent food, as are angle-worms and snails. Ducklings are quite as good as chickens at devouring insects, and nothing seems to harm them but rose-bugs, against which they should be jealously guarded. For this reason they should be kept away from grape-vines and other plants specially attractive to these insects. As the ducklings grow older they may have more liberty and a greater variety of food. If they have not plenty of grass, its place should be supplied by lettuce, onions, cabbage, or other green succulent food. If you desire exhibition birds of the largest size, it is particularly important that the ducklings should be fed regularly, and at frequent intervals, having all the food they can digest. Five times a day is none too frequent feeding. We have usually succeeded quite as well with ducks as with chickens in a village yard. When grown, we give them a larger range.

AN ARTIFICIAL DUCK-POND.

Ducks and geese may be raised successfully without any pond or stream; yet some prefer to give them an abundance of water, and such can make an artificial pond on the plan shown at Fig. 81. This is a wooden box ten inches deep and four feet square, or it may be two feet wide and six or eight feet long. This is set in the ground, except the down-hill side, which is partly exposed, and provided with a short spout placed within half an inch of the top, to carry off superfluous water. A peg is inserted at the bottom for drawing off the water when desired. Water may be conducted to the box by a pipe from a spring, underdrain, small brook, or from the well, by sinking a half-barrel between the pump and pond, and filling it with water every day or two, and so graduating the flow that it will merely drop from the barrel through the pipe into the wooden box.

Pekin ducks are white, with a yellowish tinge to the under part of the feathers; their wings are a little less than medium length, as compared with other varieties; they make as little effort to fly as the large Asiatic fowls, and they can be as easily kept in inclosures. Their beaks are yellow, necks long, legs short and red.

They are very large, and uniform in size, weighing at four months old about twelve pounds to the pair. They are very hardy, not minding severe weather. Water to drink seems to be all they require to bring them to perfect development.

THE CARE OF DUCKS.

Ducks are a very pleasant feature of farm-yard surroundings. In the last of winter and early spring they are sociable and busy enough, especially on warm days, and begin to lay very early. The duck almost always lays her egg between six and nine o'clock. So the flock must be kept shut up until all have laid. We have found ducks to do better if they can be confined at night, in winter, in a shed where the horse manure is thrown out, than anywhere else. The heaps of manure heat somewhat, and the ducks enjoy the warmth. It makes them lay early, and the eggs are not likely to freeze if we get severe "snaps." Barley and oats are excellent feed for ducks. If these or any grains are thrown into a shallow tub, or trough, they will soak and be all the better relished. Pekin Ducks are among the best layers, by far the best in our experience, laying not unfrequently sixty to eighty eggs each, in the spring, and often again in the autumn, if the weather is warm. If ducks are not confined at night, they will make nests in some hedge-row or secluded spot difficult to find, and one will become broody after laying sixteen to twenty eggs, or as soon as she has a good clutch. When confined as we suggested, they rarely make nests, but drop their eggs about anywhere. Ducks are very fond of water-cress, and if they have access to the water-cress bed at the spring, there will soon be none left for the salad-bowl. Wire netting, a foot in height, will form an effectual barrier.

PEKIN DUCKS.

The Pekin Duck was unknown in this country or Europe previous to the spring of 1873. The following is a brief account of their importation. Mr. McGrath, of the firm of Fogg & Co., engaged in the Japan and China trade, in one of his excursions in China first saw these ducks at the city of Pekin, and from their large size, thought them a small breed of geese. He succeeded in purchasing a number of the eggs, and carried them to Shanghai, where, placing them under hens, he in due time obtained fifteen ducklings sufficiently mature to ship in charge of Mr. James E. Palmer, who was about returning to America. He offered Mr. P. one half the birds that he should bring to port alive, and the latter, accepting the offer, took charge of them. Six ducks and three drakes survived the voyage of 124 days, and were landed in New York on the 13th of March, 1873. Leaving three ducks and two drakes, consigned to parties in New York, to be sent to Mr. McGrath's family (who never received them, as they were killed and eaten in the city), Mr. P. took the three remaining ducks and drake to his home at Wequetequoc, in Stonington, Conn. They soon recovered from the effects of their long voyage, and commenced laying the latter part of March, and continued to lay until the last of July. They are very prolific, the three ducks laying about 325 eggs.

The ducks are white, with a yellowish tinge to the under part of the feathers; their wings are a little less than medium length, as compared with other varieties; they make as little effort to fly as the large Asiatic fowls, and they can be as easily kept in enclosures. Their beaks are yellow; necks long; legs short and red. When the eggs are hatched under hens, the ducklings come out of the shell much stronger if the eggs are dampened every day (after the first fifteen days) in water a little above blood heat and replaced under the hen.

The ducks are very large, and uniform in size, weighing at four months old about twelve pounds to the pair. They appear to be very hardy, not minding severe weather. Water to drink seems to be all they require to bring them to perfect development.

I was more successful in rearing them with only a dish filled to the depth of one inch with water, than were those who had the advantages of a pond and running stream.

AYLESBURY DUCKS.

White occurring without intermixture of other color in the hair or feathers of animals and fowls is evidence of change effected by domestication. This color, or lack of color, becomes a very persistent characteristic. The accompanying engraving of Aylesbury Ducks represents one of the most beautiful of the white breeds of poultry. All white fowls are beautiful and attractive. We have white breeds of every kind of domestic fowl, and they all have such notable excellencies that their admirers claim for each that it is the best of its kind. This is noticeable in white geese, which have the best plumage; white turkeys are most domestic, and white barn-door fowls are most prolific. Aylesbury Ducks are claimed to be more prolific and to fatten more rapidly for market than other large breeds. This variety undoubtedly originated in the vicinity of Aylesbury, England, where large numbers are still raised annually for the London market. Its characteristics are distinctly marked, namely: Abundant but close-fitting plumage of the purest white; a beak of peculiar form, being long, straight, and broad, and set on a line with the forehead; most noticeable, however, from its being of a distinct flesh-color; it sometimes inclines to buff, but this is objectionable. The most delicate pink (as an English breeder enthusiastically said to the writer, "pink as a lady's nail") is the color preferred; the legs are of a light orange color. Ducks and drakes are almost precisely alike, the latter distinguished only by the curling feathers of the tail and by the voice, or lack of voice.

This is an old and well-established breed, and in favorable locations breeds very true. Breeders so located find it is not difficult to obtain the pink bills without stain of yellow or blemish of dark streaks or specks. This is supposed to depend upon the purity of the water, and on the gravelly bottom of the brooks with which their bills are constantly brought in contact. Exposure to the sun tans them, and, from some not well-known cause, it is almost impossible to obtain perfect bills in many places, though the birds grow large and fine.

It is customary in and near Aylesbury to confine the ducks in warm houses early in the season, and to induce the earliest possible laying, that the young ducks may be marketed very early in the season, and high prices secured. They come to the market just at a season when game and other poultry are scarce and high. Now, when the Aylesburys are removed from their home surroundings, and, as in this country, are treated like other kinds of ducks, they retain this tendency to lay, and hatch a brood early in mid-winter, only for the first generation from importation, even then to a less degree than the imported birds show it. The tendency to lay very early would no doubt be maintained if it were encouraged as it is at home. In regard to the care of ducks, it is well to observe that the more a variety is changed by domestication, the more attention they need, and usually the more profit they yield. Many common ducks lay a clutch of perhaps 20 small eggs; in sitting, cover half or more, and hatch them out, while the Aylesbury Duck will lay 60 eggs or more, but until she begins to show a tendency to sit, usually a week or ten days before she sits, she makes a sort of nest, and there she deposits her eggs. The only way to secure all the eggs is to shut up the ducks at night. They will usually lay an egg apiece between dawn and eight o'clock; and as soon as each has laid, all may be let out. They all march straight for the water; and if let out too soon, some eggs will be almost surely found in the bottom of the pond. Ducks are voracious and almost omnivorous feeders; they are fond of grass and water plants, water-cress especially, and are diligent foragers for snails and the little shell-fish of fresh-water streams, ponds, and swamps; and, besides, on dry land they are indefatigable insect-hunters, young ducks being often very useful in a vegetable garden, where they gather and destroy many plant-pests.

A pair of Aylesbury Ducks fit for exhibition ought

to weigh at least 12 pounds; in England they often reach 16 pounds to the pair; and are occasionally heavier by one or two pounds, thus almost equaling the weight of the heaviest specimens of Rouen Ducks.

ROUEN DUCKS.

There is a prevalent belief among farmers that ducks are not profitable poultry. This arises naturally from several causes. The habits of indolence which some possess—the tendency not to hunt their food, but to depend upon being fed and the scraps which they pick up about the house—lead farmers to contrast them unfavorably with the wandering turkeys, which find their living and rear their young often in the woods, depending only in winter upon the farmer for their food; and scarcely more favorably with dunghill fowls, which during the summer months require but little food except what they hunt for about the farm. The ducks, besides, though some kinds are excellent layers, are heedless birds, exposing themselves, their eggs, and young to crows, rats, turtles, and other vermin, dropping their eggs about, shifting their place of laying if disturbed, inconstant as sitters, and chilling their young by taking them too soon and too often to the water. Still, all these objections may be obviated, in a measure, and ducks really pay very well both in flesh and eggs for the amount of food they consume.

The duck is an omnivorous animal—eating almost everything vegetable and animal that comes in its way. Insects of all kinds, worms, polliwigs, fish, shellfish (dead or alive), meat, even that which is partly decomposed, and many green vegetables, grass, seeds, grain, etc. Withal, its appetite is voracious; hence it grows

Fig. 88.—PAIR OF ROUEN DUCKS.

(231)

rapidly and fattens easily. The common tame duck is supposed to have descended from the wild Mallard duck, *Anas boshas*, common to this country and Europe. It breeds freely with this species, and also with several other species of wild duck ; in some cases the progeny is capable of reproduction of its kind, in others mule-birds or "mongrels" result. The fact that a very different class of birds is produced where the Mallards are crossed with other species and where the common duck is so crossed, with other points of difference, throws some doubt on the assertion that the Mallard is the parent of our common ducks. Besides, efforts to domesticate the Mallard have not been successful as a general thing. We have, however, many wild ducks capable of domestication, and the experiment ought to be well tried with all, for thus our stock of domestic poultry may be essentially increased and improved.

The Rouen breed is the most highly esteemed of all domestic ducks by many duck breeders. Its habits are quiet, and so it does not wander about and get lost, as ducks do. It attains a great weight, and is unsurpassed as a layer. An English writer reports that he has frequently known a pair of young drakes 9 or 10 weeks old to weigh 12 lbs. Sundry writers report very remarkable laying performances of the Rouen ducks. One laid an egg a day for 85 days ; three ducks from February to July laid 334 eggs, besides a few soft ones and five double eggs. One of these laid every morning for 92 days. The young ducks often lay in autumn a good clutch of eggs, and it not unfrequently occurs that a duck which is a first-rate layer will manifest no tendency to sit. This variety of ducks has, in common with many other kinds, great beauty of plumage, which varies somewhat in different individuals. The drakes are heavier than the ducks, but the difference is slight in comparison with the disparity between the sexes in most varieties.

The beautiful green heads and necks of the drakes, iridescent with purple and copper hues, set off with a clean white collar and claret-colored vest, give them a distinguished air which the various colors and distinct markings of the back and wings does not detract from. The females are brown, each feather being marked with black, which gives them a speckled look.

The only variety which really rivals the Rouen as a useful and economical birds is the Aylesbury. These, a purely white English variety, are beautiful birds and highly esteemed in the markets of Great Britain, as also in the United States, where they are known. They are good layers and nurses, not noisy; good feeders, and by some decidedly preferred to the Rouen. The eggs are white, sometimes inclining to blue, while those of the Rouen duck are blue, with thick, strong shells; of the two the Rouen has the reputation of being most hardy. Where ducks are raised for breeders, it is a practice (founded perhaps on prejudice) to set ducks upon their own eggs; but if the young are wanted for market simply, the eggs are put under hens. Hens will hatch a clutch of duck's some two days quicker than ducks will, but it is thought that the young have not so good constitutions. Young ducks raised for market often get injured by being allowed to go freely to the water. They grow faster and stronger if they only have enough to drink, at least for several weeks.

CHAPTER XXII.

ORNAMENTAL POULTRY.

THE PEA-FOWL.

Although the pea-fowl is well known as a bird of fine feathers, few persons are acquainted with its natural history and real merits. It is a good table fowl, and as easily reared as the turkey; still it is rarely seen on a farm or country place, and then only as an ornament. This bird is a native of Asia, from whence have come nearly all our gallinaceous fowls, the turkey excepted. In the time of Solomon, it was an article of merchandise, and was brought with ivory and apes from Tarshish to Judea. One species of pea-fowl was found by an English traveler, Colonel Sykes, abounding in a part of India, where large flocks were kept about the native temples. Another Eastern traveler relates that from 1,200 to 1,500 were seen by him in the passes of the mountain, within sight at one time; and he speaks in extravagant terms of the brilliancy of their plumage. There are three distinct genera, which include several species and varieties, such as the Crested, the Black-shouldered, the Javan, the Japan, the Iris, the Thibet, the Malay, etc. All the domesticated sorts are surpassed by the wild ones in beauty. Culver says of the pea-fowl: "We find in its incomparable robe, united, all the brilliant colors which we admire separately in other birds; we find all that glistens in the rainbow, that sparkles in the mine, the azure and golden tints of the heavens, and the emerald of the field." White, the naturalist, found that the feathers of the train do not belong to the tail, but that they grow upon the back, the real tail feathers being short, stiff, and brown, about six inches long, and serve as a prop to support the immense train. By a peculiar muscular action, the long train feathers can be erected and spread, and their shafts made to strike together and produce a chattering noise. The Pied peacock is white upon the wings, belly, and breast; the rest of the plumage is as showy as in the other species. Pure white birds are very rare, and highly valued; but from the absence of the gorgeous coloring of the common kinds, they suffer greatly in contrast with the latter. It is not until the second year that the difference between the sexes becomes apparent. The bird lives from 20 to 25 years, and reaches maturity slowly. The third year the train of the cock becomes developed, and it is only when it exhibits its full coloring that he is ready to be mated with three or four hens.

The pea-hen lays her eggs on alternate days, and when she has produced five or six she will incubate, unless the eggs have been removed. She makes her nest upon the ground, in a secluded place, beneath the shelter of low bushes, long grass, or weeds. The maternal instinct is well developed in some hens; in other hens it is so lacking that they even destroy their own young, or leave them to perish from neglect. The period of incubation is from 24 to 29 days. The pea-fowls have strong local attachments, and they rarely leave the place where they have been reared and fed. They are sensible of kind treatment, and will become very tame when gently used and petted. They have a habit of roosting high, and will choose an elevated place on the top of the highest tree or buildings to which they can gain access. When but three days old, the chicks are able to reach a roost two or three feet high; and if they can mount from one step to another, they will follow the old birds to their highest roosting places. The birds are naturally shy, and their treatment must be regulated accordingly. The proper feed for the young pea-chicks consists of hard boiled eggs, cracked wheat, coarse oatmeal, and bread-crumbs; and they will soon hunt after and consume insects and worms of all kinds. It is necessary to protect the young birds from wet and cold, and they require the same care which is needed for young turkeys.

TRAINING PEA-FOWLS TO STAY AT HOME.

At "Rose Lawn," Paterson, N. J., there is a flock of pea-fowls—half a dozen or more. They are confined, or rather kept, in a lot of perhaps two acres in extent, which has a high fence of wire net, and where they are associated with a small herd of deer and farm-yard poultry of all sorts. They fly into the tops of the apple-trees to roost, but never fly out of the enclosure. Seeing them so apparetly contented, day after day, and knowing well the restless habits of the bird, especially the male, which generally makes himself a nuisance to the whole neighborhood within half a mile, this domestic trait of these birds interested us, and we learned that if one flies out, he is condemned to wear a ball and chain, or rather a cord and block, for several days. It is thus applied: Strong list of woolen goods, or other soft, strong band, is passed about the leg of the peacock, so that it cannot tighten, and to this is attached a block of hickory or other heavy wood, weighing three or four pounds. The block should be round or conical, and should have a hole through it lengthways, and the cord should pass through this, and be well knotted at the end. It must turn in the block so as to prevent kinking. These gorgeous fowls would be much more frequently kept if it were known that they might be so easily trained.

JAPANESE BANTAMS.

These quaint little creatures weigh about a pound and a quarter each. The plumage is white, excepting some

Fig. 89.—JAPANESE BANTAMS.

of the wing feathers, the tail, and sometimes the tips of the neck feathers, which are black. The legs are bright yellow. The tail is the most curious part of this breed,

Fig. 90.—SEBASTOPOL GOOSE.

being large, and carried so erect as to nearly touch the head. The legs are so short as to be almost invisible, and this gives the birds a curious creeping sort of gait The little hens are exemplary mothers, and one of them, with a brood of tiny chicks, would be the delight of a boy or girl, as well as attractive pets for old folks. This breed has the virtue, rare amongst bantams, of being exceedingly peaceable and quiet.

ORNAMENTAL WATER-FOWLS.

In this country we have much to learn in the way of utilizing natural waters, whether streams, springs, or ponds. Any place, anywhere, be it a farm, large or small, or merely a country-seat, has its value greatly enhanced by the possession of water, whether running or still. Of the money value of such water, whether for stock, irrigation, or as motive power, we do not propose to speak just now. The value of water in these respects is as far from being appreciated as it is in its ornamental aspects. We know of one body of water—a small pond, which is so treated by its owner as to be both profitable and ornamental. It is a conspicuous object from the road, and being not far from the house, its surroundings are planted with a view to ornamental effect. The water is at the same time made useful as the pasture-ground for a fine collection of water-fowl. The flock contains some birds raised for the table, but is largely of the kinds known as ornamental, and these are made profitable; the place being in a populous vicinity, the birds do their own advertising, and there is a sufficient demand for all the increase. The practical part of the establishment, including the breeding-houses, coops, etc., is at some distance from the pond and hidden from view by a screen of evergreens planted for the purpose. Among the birds regarded as both ornamental and useful are the

---

SEBASTOPOL GEESE.

This is a most peculiar variety of the goose, one of its peculiarities being that no one knows why it is called "Sebastopol." It is said to come from the Black Sea country, but even this is doubtful. The characteristic of the breed consists in having a large share of its pure white feathers, especially of the back, wings, and tail, very long, lax, curled, waved, and frizzled. These feathers give the birds a somewhat bedraggled look, when on land, but impart a most elegant appearance when they are on the water. For the rest, though rarely weighing ten pounds, they are useful table birds, are hardy, prolific, and good sitters and mothers.

THE WHISTLING DUCKS

are among the ornamental ducks, in which beauty of plumage is regarded rather than weight. They are from South America, and there appear to be several sub-varieties, distinguished mainly by the color of the bill, but all agree in having a peculiar whistling note. All are very domestic, and remarkably quaint and amusing in their habits and movements. The birds shown in the engraving are known as the "Widow Whistler" and the "White-faced Whistler." Their general color is a light shade of chocolate, with black below; the head, neck, and bill are also black, making the white face all the more conspicuous and very attractive.

Fig. 91.—WHISTLING DUCKS.

(243)

THE AMERICAN WOOD DUCK—OR SUMMER DUCK.

We have in this country many beautiful varieties of wild ducks, some of which we know are capable of domestication, and more which have not been experimented with. One of the former is the "Summer duck" of Southern and the "Wood duck" of the Northern States. Either name is appropriate, for it is the only duck which

Fig. 92.—AMERICAN WOOD DUCK.

remains with us during breeding season, except now and then a stray pair of Mallards, and perhaps a pair of one or two other kinds are very rarely seen; and its natural haunts are the deep quiet woods far from the dwellings of men. The bird is rather rare in New England, especially so in the Eastern part, more plenty in New York, and abundant in Pennsylvania, and to the westward and south, wherever a wooded country offers pools and secluded river and lake margins, close to which it delights to make its nest and rear its young. The engraving represents a beautiful bird, but one not familiar with these ducks would hardly credit the correctness of an accurate description of its colors. The bill and legs are red, the dark feathers of the head exhibit gorgeous steel-blue, coppery and green iridescence, and in some lights are jetty, velvety black, or purple. The white feathers on the head and neck, in the queue-like tuft of the back of head, and on the shoulders, wing covers and sides are all clear, vivid dashes in every case contrasted with black bands or bordering of dark, nearly black feathers. The back shows the brilliant rainbow hues and metallic colors of the head, while the breast is of a delicate wine color, spotted with white, and the belly white, shading into ash-color on the sides. These colors belong to the drakes; the ducks are similar, but much less showy. In Pennsylvania and northward they pair in April or May, and the female brings off her brood of eight to fifteen in June. They migrate just before winter sets in and are very likely to return to the same locality. The flesh of the young birds are highly esteemed. During the winter they go into the Southern States, and are there seen in large flocks.

This duck has been repeatedly domesticated, so as to be as familiar as any denizens of the farm yard. The best way to get them is to find the nests, which are usually in a hollow tree not far from the water (they use an old woodpecker's or gray squirrel's hole if they can find one big enough), and transfer the fresh eggs to a sitting hen, or else take the very young ducks as soon as they are hatched.

CHAPTER XXIII.

THEORY AND PRACTICE.

SYSTEMATIC CROSS-BREEDING.

The continual advocacy of fancy poultry for common farm use is an error. The poultry papers, and most agricultural papers, advise the breeding of certain pure breeds, as if they possessed merits far superior to the barn-door fowls and common poultry. This is a mistake. No one advocates the use of thoroughbred horses, well-bred trotters, pure Percherons or Clydes, pure-bred pigs, or sheep, or cattle, to the exclusion of common ones, but farmers are urged to improve their common stock by breeding up, by gradually introducing better blood and breeding, with some definite aim. Thus, our common mixed sheep, which are regular breeders, good mothers, and have plenty of milk, are crossed with pure rams of one of the established breeds. If size is wanted, with long wool, the Cotswold is perhaps employed; if the wool is to be improved in fineness without so much reference to the mutton, one of the Merino breeds will be selected; while if early lambs of fine quality are desired, one of the Down breeds is chosen by the raiser. This is precisely the course which should be followed by farmers in poultry-raising. The advantage of grading up common poultry is, however, not so profitable in most cases as cross-breeding. This is, properly, the interbreeding of two pure varieties. We have, however, usually no pure breed of fowls upon the farm, and of course wish to utilize those which we have. Therefore the first thing to do is to grade up the flock. After two or three years, when they have the looks and qualities of pure-breds, the hens may be crossed with cocks of another breed, and then most of the advantages of cross-breeding will be realized. In this use of pure-bred cocks which we recommend, no male bird should run with the same flock more than two years. If he is healthy and vigorous, and his progeny of the first year take strongly after him, in form as well as feather, he may well be kept the second year to run with pullets of his own get. After three years the blood of the original flock will be reduced to one-eighth; after four years to one-sixteenth. One may have a flock of hens which have been carelessly bred, and into which no fresh blood has been introduced for years. They are small, hardy, active, fair layers, good sitters and mothers, and get their own living all summer—but the garden suffers. How can the flock be improved? This, we conceive, is the question which may be put by ninety-nine in a hundred of the keepers of hens in the country. The answer suggests itself, but first we should know whether eggs, or broilers, or full-grown fowls for market (chickens in autumn or winter) pay best. The farmer must treat his flock of hens exactly as he would his flock of sheep or his herd of cows, or other stock; that is, secure the use of full-blood males having the desired characteristics. Thus, if he wishes eggs, he will buy cocks of some *one* of those breeds famous for the number of eggs the hens lay. Size and beauty of eggs may be an object, or simply a large number may be most desirable. The French breeds and the Spanish usually have large eggs; Leghorns, eggs of medium size; Hamburgs lay many but small eggs; while all are persistent layers of beautiful white eggs. The half-bloods, as a whole, will take after the pure breed in a good measure, and in so far may be said to be an improvement upon the old stock. The second year the three-quarter bloods will closely resemble pure-bred ones; some will only be distinguished from pure-bloods by an expert, while others will show their dung-hill origin very clearly, and yet, as layers, these may be the very best. So improvement goes on. The flock will in two or three years assume the appearance of "fancy" poultry of the breed selected with which to produce the improvement. The question naturally arises, Will they be improved?—be better and more profitable than they were before? Perhaps not for all uses,—but as layers, yes. The hens will lay more eggs; they will be less inclined to sit; if they sit at all, they will probably be broody only for a few days, and as producers of eggs no doubt the flock will be more satisfactory. Should one of the French breeds have been selected—say the Houdans or Crevecœurs—the change and improvement in the flock will be very marked. As to the number of eggs, a flock crossed and graded up with Leghorns will surpass them, but the eggs of the French grades will exceed the others in size and possibly total weight. Besides, the birds will be larger, and very much superior for the table. In fact, were one to set out to grade up a flock of common fowls to produce the best table fowls for autumn and winter, he could hardly do better than take the Houdan or Crevecœur, which are large, have superior flesh, white skins, and are persistent layers of large white eggs. They are, however, less hardy than the Leghorns.

MULTIPLICATION OF BREEDS OF POULTRY.

With our domestic animals, as with wine and cheese, the value of a breed depends in some measure upon its age. If breeders realized this, there would be less running after the so-called breeds which spring up every year or two. At the time the Leghorns were first brought to this country, they were a most unpromising lot, as we remember them, but they had elements of great value. White seemed to predominate, and the single-combed white fowls were separated from the others and carefully bred. It was several years before a fixed breed was established, even with this excellent foundation. The foundation was good, because all the birds had the same general characteristics, which were peculiar and valuable, such as were possessed by none of the then existing favorite breeds. So when the Leghorns were introduced, with the uniform points of a fancier's fowl, they became at once great favorites and had deserved success. Then this excellent and unique breed was made to carry forward with it, towards popularity, a number of allied breeds, all decidedly inferior to it—Browns, Blacks, Dominiques, etc.—and now it seems this breed, which properly affiliates with the Spanish, is to be Hamburgized and given a rose comb, and for aught we know blue legs. It is true that irregular rose combs occasionally appeared in the original stock; but they were regarded as abnormal. Now it is really absurd to introduce them for no merit, but simply to add another breed, or three or four breeds perhaps, to our already too long list of the Leghorn family.

Some time ago a cross was made, which had Dominique plumage, with large size, hardiness, small bone, yellow skin, quick growth, and the characteristics of a good "general purpose," fowl. This is the Plymouth Rock variety. It was not a breed, but a cross. However, after years of breeding to a fixed standard, it is now worthy of being received as an established breed. But it is still shaky. Left alone a few years, it will revert, more or less; and in the best regulated families, black fowls are constantly putting in an appearance.

As if one such breed were not enough, another has been introduced, with no merit, that we are aware of, that the Plymouths have not. It is a speckled, mongrel-looking breed in the yard, though magnificent in the pictures ; and yet the whole world of American poultry people seem to be going daft over it, probably because it is so well advertised. It is pretty near a crime to admit these mongrel breeds, if they may be so called, to "the standard," and give them the approval of the united poultry breeders of this country. We have now breeds enough, unless somebody will get up a breed of fowls that will lay buff eggs, and will not sit. That would be both novel and useful. It would be better for poultry fanciers to try to improve the breeds we now have, and to learn by experimenting how to best use them in crosses.

A WOMAN'S POULTRY KEEPING.

Poultry are never better cared for than when under the charge of women, especially during the hatching and brooding season. The following letter is full of common-sense hints:

Farmers do not appreciate chickens at near their full value. In fact, they are frequently grumbling about them for one reason or another, though they are very fond of fresh eggs, the cakes and puddings that require eggs in their composition, or a pair of fine roast fowl on their table once a week at least. I think that chickens —I keep no other kind of poultry now—pay more, in proportion to their cost, than anything on a farm. I have received many compliments from local buyers on the fine quality of my fowls, but they will not give me one cent more per pound than they do for an inferior lot. The farmers get more for the best-fed fowls in the large cities to which they ship their poultry. I have only a rough board hen-house, twelve by sixteen feet, with strips of clap-boards over the cracks to keep the wind out. A window with a shutter in the south gable end, and a large sliding-door in the side facing the east, are the only ventilators. Over one hundred hens were kept in this cheap house last winter, terribly cold as it was, without being frost-bitten. A few hens laid all winter, and a large number began to lay on the first of February. I have a much smaller house close by, where hens lay and set. I find this detached house better for them, and more convenient for me. Both houses are whitewashed inside, and have gravel floors. In the sleeping-house the roosts are made like ladders, and very slanting to allow the fowls to go up and down easily. Early in the morning I take the setting hens off their nests and feed them before opening the door of the larger house to give the others their liberty. The sitters never stay from their nests over ten or fifteen minutes, and so are soon out of the way of the rest. I have a long row of coops (made by myself), where I keep the hens that hvae hatched until the little ones get quite strong.

I always feed the chicks curds and corn-meal mixed three times a day. I have a long, narrow, shallow trough, always full of milk or whey, where all the chickens, young and old, can drink at will. This, I suppose, is the reason that they are always fat and healthy, and why the hens lay so well. I have three feeding coops for the young chickens. One with the slats just far enough apart to admit very little chicks. The next in size for those whose mothers have left them, and the largest coop is for full-feathered chickens. In this way the little ones are not bullied out of their share of the feed. I have another house eight by ten feet inclosed with a lath fence, in a small yard fourteen feet square, where I place those chickens I wish to fatten for eating at home and for market. I can make them very fat in ten days, at the most, on corn-meal, curds, and boiled rice. They have all the milk they can drink—it requires very little to satisfy them—and chopped cabbage or the leaves of the wild plantain, which they devour greedily, and plenty of fine gravel and charcoal. My spring chickens average four pounds in weight in August, when they are fat and very good eating. They are mostly Plymouth Rocks, the cocks all thoroughbred, with a slight cross of Buff Cochin in some of the hens. Last year I had but seventy-two hens in the spring, and I made, from February to the middle of December, one hundred and eighteen dollars from eggs and chickens sold, and we ate besides ninety-seven chickens, and from eighteen to twenty eggs a day. The cost of their food during the year was twenty-six dollars. If properly taken care of, chickens always pay on a farm, where they can have a good range. We have only pasture land near our house and barns, so they are not troublesome in the grain fields, or in the garden.

AUTUMN MANAGEMENT OF POULTRY.

Flocks of poultry require to be carefully managed in autumn to be made profitable. If the male birds have not been separated, this should be done early; they are only an annoyance, and an injury to the hens, and prevent them from laying as many eggs as they would otherwise do. The young cockerels that are fit for sale, should be disposed of; others should be shut in a yard by themselves, and fed for the market. The best of the early pullets should now begin to lay, and if of good breeds, and well fed, will continue to lay until the cold weather. Old hens are unprofitable, and should be weeded out, and this is the time to do it if they were not sold in the spring or used for pot-pie during the summer. They will never be heavier and fatter than they are now, and the feed they will consume will be all loss. For fattening fowls, the following arrangement will be found effective: A long, low box (a shoe box, laid upon its side, answers very well), is lathed up and down in the front, leaving an opening all along the front, a bar being fitted across the box, three inches above the bottom. This bottom opening is to clean out the box with a scraper, once every day; after which dry earth is thrown in. This box will hold six fowls, and a feeding trough, and a water can should be fitted in front. A number of boxes may be tiered one over the other, and when the fowls have fed, the front should be covered and darkened by hanging bagging over it. This will keep the fowls quiet. Two weeks of this treatment will fatten them. The finest flesh is made by feeding corn-meal and boiled potatoes, mixed with skimmed milk, quite thick, and four feeds a day should be given. Fowls are best slaughtered and dressed as follows: A barrel is provided, with a number of nails driven in around the open edge. A number of loops of twine, about six inches long, are also provided. The bird is fastened by noosing the loop around the legs, and is hung in the barrel, head downwards. The head is then taken in the left hand, and a sharp pointed knife is pushed through the throat, close to the vertebra, and drawn forward so as to cut the throat clear through, by which sensation is at once arrested, and the fowl bleeds to death rapidly and painlessly. Being confined in the barrel, the splashing from the fluttering is avoided, and everything is done in a cleanly and easy manner. Dry picking is preferred by the marketmen, but the extra price will hardly pay for the trouble over the scalding of the fowls, and the easier picking in that way. To scald a fowl, take a pail three-quarters full of boiling water, and plunge the bird into it, drawing it up and down a few times. Keep the water up to the scalding heat by adding a quart of boiling water occasionally.

INDEX.

	PAGE		PAGE
Annex to poultry house	60	Brooding pen for hens	52
Autumn management	253	Caponizing, how done	93
Bantam fowls	107	Instruments	95, 96
Barrel hen's nest	37	Charcoal and stimulants	106
Breed, best for market	8	Chicken coop complete	54
For broilers	10	Box	57
For early roasters	9	Barrel	58
For late roasters	9	Chicks, brooders for early	62
Breeds, multiplication of	249	Chicks, care of	54
Popular	121	Chicks, raising early	60
Breeds of Fowls:		Color of skin not affected by feed	8
American	168	Common sense	101
American Dominiques	172	Cold latitudes, wintering fowls	113
American Javas	177	Crates, folding	43
Asiatic	123	Crook for catching fowls	117
Black Cochin	131	Crops raised for poultry	109
Black-red Game	144	Cross-breeding, advantage of	100
Black Spanish	154	Cross-breeding, systematic	247
Brown Leghorns	160	Disease, defence against	187
Buff Cochins	131	Diseases of poultry	178
Crevecœur	165	Bumble-foot	186
Dark Brahmas	127	Chicken-pox	181
Duck wing Game	140	Cholera, the	181
European	136	Distemper	178
French	161	Egg-bound	186
Hamburgs	145	Egg-eating	184
Houdan	161	Feather-eating	185
Langshans	131	Feathers, loss of	186
Light Brahmas	123	Gapes, the	185
Games	139	Pip, the	185
Partridge Cochins	128	Roup, the	178
Plymouth Rocks	168	Scabby legs	183
Polish	149	Duck house	220
Silver-gray Dorkings	136	Duck-mothers	219
White Cochins	131	Duck-raising	218, 225
White-crested white Polish	150	Ducks need little water	223
White Dorkings	137	Pekins as layers	220, 236
White Leghorns	156	Ducks, American Wood	245
Wyandottes	173	Aylesbury	227
Brooders for chicks	62–75	Pekin	226
Brooder house	75	Rouen	230

	PAGE		PAGE
Ducks—*continued*.		Nest boxes—*continued*.	
Whistling	242	Sliding, through partition	34
Egg testing	47	Pinned together	36
Crate	90	Nest of woven wire	38
Ladle	39	In a barrel	37
Eggs, "caudling"	48	Nests for egg-eating hens	37
For market	86	Tidy	40
In Great Britain and in the United States	91	New York dressed-poultry law	82
		Pasturing Fowls	118
Liming	86–89	Parasites	189
Packing in barrels	87	Pea-fowl	235
Packing for winter	89	Trained to stay at home	237
To secure in winter	115	Perches, handy	31
Vat for pickling	90	Poultry conveniences	81
Fattening ration	11	Dressing and stuffing	81
Feather-bone	84	Dressing—New England method	83
Feathers, save the	84		
Feeding-pen for chicks	59	Ornamental	235
Feed-trough, cleanly	41	Special food crops	109
Fowls, egg-bound	186	Raising	7
Egg-eating	184	When to market	80
Feather-eating	185	Poultry houses	13
Green food for	105	Building materials for	25
Losing feathers	186	C. H Colburn's	21
Management and feed	10	Half under ground	25
Selecting and selling	115	Portable	27
White-skinned preferred in Philadelphia, etc	8	Very cheap	13
		Very complete	21
Yellow-skinned preferred in New England	8	Warm	14
		Poultry-keeping as a business	98
Game fowls at fairs	144	Money made by	99
Green food	105	Poultry-management, hints	101
Geese, Embden	215	Poultryman's crook	117
Plucking	216	Poultry-yard, common-sense in	101
Sebastopol	242	Ration for fattening	11
Toulouse origin	215	Ration, salt in	104
Varieties of	212	Roosts, low	32
Goose-raising	210	Salt in the ration	104
Incubation, artificial	65	Samuels on market breeds	8
Incubation, natural	46	Shipping crates, folding	43
Incubators, directions for running	72	Sitting-box, secure	50
		Sitting hens, care of	49
Hot water	68	Stimulants, use of	106
How to make	69	Stone for a poultry-house	83
Sawdust packing	71	Theory and practice	247
Self-regulators	68	Turkey nests	203
Success and Failure with	86	Raising	193
Thermometer for	74	Roosts	195
Indian-meal dough	11	Turkeys, bronze	194
Japanese Bantams	238	Early broods	204
Large birds, how to raise	119	Fattening	196
Lice on hens	189	Feeding the chicks	206
Prevention of	117	Hints about	203
Louse-eggs on feathers	189	Loss of weight in dressing	208
Males, importance of pure	122	Setting the hens	205
Marketing poultry	80	Wild, habits of	198
Market Law, New York	82	Water-fountain, pneumatic	41
Nest box, locked	39	Water-fountain for winter	42
Secure	50	Water-fowls, ornamental	241
With roller in front	40	Wintering fowls in cold latitudes	113
Nest boxes	33–35	Women as poultry-raisers	251

ALPHABETICAL CATALOGUE
— OF —

O. Judd Co., David W. Judd, Pres't,

PUBLISHERS AND IMPORTERS OF

All Works pertaining to Rural Life.

751 Broadway, New York.

Agriculture, Horticulture, Etc.

FARM AND GARDEN.

Allen, R. L. and L. F. New American Farm Book............$ 2.50
American Farmer's Hand Book............ .... 2.50
Asparagus Culture. Flex. Cloth.... .... .50
Bamford, C. E. Silk Culture. Paper........................ .30
Barry, P. The Fruit Garden. New and Revised Edition........... 2.00
Bommer. Method of Making Manures .... .25
Brackett. Farm Talk. Paper 50c. Cloth .... .75
Brill. Farm-Gardening and Seed-Growing... .... 1.00
——— Cauliflowers....... .... .20
Broom-Corn and Brooms. Paper .... .50

O. JUDD CO.'S ALPHABETICAL CATALOGUE.

Curtis on Wheat Culture. Paper................................. .50
Emerson and Flint. Manual of Agriculture............... 1.50
Farm Conveniences 1.50
Farming for Boys... 1.25
Farming for Profit... 3.75
Fitz. Sweet Potato Culture. New, Revised and Enlarged Edition...... .60
Flax Culture. Paper.. .30
French. Farm Drainage... 1.50
Fuller, A. S. Practical Forestry................................ 1.50
Gregory. On Cabbages.. .30
——— On Carrots, Mangold Wurtzels, etc................. .30
——— On Fertilizers... .40
——— On Onion Raising...................................... .30
——— On Squashes.. .30
Harlan. Farming with Green Manures 1.00
Harris. Insects Injurious to Vegetation. Plain $4. Col'd Engravings. 6.50
Harris, Joseph. Gardening for Young and Old................. 1.25
——— Talks on Manures. New and Revised Edition... 1.75
Henderson, Peter. Gardening for Pleasure.................... 1.50
——— Gardening for Profit. New and **Enlarged** Edition. 2.00
——— Garden and Farm Topics................................ 1.50
Henderson & Crozier. How the Farm Pays.................... 2.50
Hop Culture. New and Revised Edition. Paper............ .30
Johnston. Agricultural Chemistry............................. 1.75
Johnson, M. W. How to Plant. Paper......................... .50
Johnson, Prof. S. W. How Crops Feed 2.00
——— How Crops Grow 2.00
Jones, B. W. The Peanut Plant. Paper....................... .50
Lawn Planting. Paper .... .25
Leland. Farm Homes, In-Doors, and Out-Doors. New Edition..... 1.50
Long, Elias A. Ornamental Gardening for Americans......... 2.00
Morton. Farmer's Calendar..................................... 5.00
Nichols. Chemistry of Farm and Sea......................... 1.25
Norton. Elements of Scientific Agriculture.................. .75
Oemler. Truck-Farming at the South........................... 1.50
Onions. How to Raise them Profitably........................ .20
Our Farm of Four Acres. Paper............................. .30
Pabor, E. Colorado as an Agricultural State................ 1.50
Pedder. Land Measurer for Farmers. Cloth.................. 60
Plant Life on the Farm.. 1.00
Quinn. Money in the Garden 1.50
Register of Rural Affairs. 9 vols. Each................... 1.50
Riley. Potato Pests. Paper.................................... .50
Robinson. Facts for Farmers................................... 5.00
Roe. Play and Profit in my Garden 1.50
Roosevelt. Five Acres Too Much................................ 1.50
Silos and Ensilage. New and Enlarged Edition............... .50
Starr. Farm Echoes.. 1.00
Stewart. Irrigation for the Farm, Garden and Orchard...... 1.50
Ten Acres Enough.. 1.00
The Illustrated Dictionary of Gardening. Vol. 1.... 5.00
The Soil of the Farm... 1.00
Thomas. Farm Implements and Machinery...................... 1.50

O. JUDD CO.'S ALPHABETICAL CATALOGUE. 3

Tim Bunker Papers; or, Yankee Farming............ 1.50
Tobacco Culture. Paper............................ .25
Treat. Injurious Insects of the Farm and Garden........... 2.00
Villes. School of Chemical Manures...................... 1.25
—— High Farming without Manures..................... .25
—— Artificial Manures............................... 6.00
Waring. Book of the Farm............................ 2.00
—— Draining for Profit and Health.................... 1.50
—— Elements of Agriculture......................... 1.00
—— Farmers' Vacation.............................. 3.00
—— Sanitary Drainage of Houses and Towns........... 2.00
—— Sanitary Condition in City and Country Dwellings.. .50
Warington. Chemistry of the Farm..................... 1.00
White. Gardening for the South...................... 2.00

FRUITS, FLOWERS, ETC.

American Rose Culturist........................... .30
American Weeds and Useful Plants................ 1.75
Boussingault. Rural Economy........................ 1.60
Chorlton. Grape-Grower's Guide...................... .75
Collier, Peter. Sorghum, its Culture and Manufacture...... 3.00
Common Sea Weeds. Boards........................ .50
Downing. Fruits and Fruit Trees of America. New Edition..... 5.00
—— Rural Essays.................................. 3.00
Elliott. Hand Book for Fruit-Growers. Paper 60c. Cloth...... 1.00
Every Woman her own Flower Gardener............ 1.00
Fern Book for Everybody........................... .50
Fuller, A. S. Grape Culturist....................... 1.50
—— Illustrated Strawberry Culturist .... .25
—— Small Fruit Culturist. New Edition................ 1.50
Fulton. Peach Culture. New and Revised Edition 1.50
Heinrich. Window Flower Garden...................... .75
Henderson, Peter. Hand Book of Plants............... 3.00
—— Practical Floriculture........................... 1.50
Hibberd, Shirley. The Amateur's Flower Garden......... 2.50
—— The Amateur's Greenhouse and Conservatory 2 50
—— The Amateur's Rose Book..................... 2.50
Hoopes. Book of Evergreens.......................... 3.00
Husmann, Prof. Geo. American Grape growing and Wine Making 1 50
Johnson. Winter Greeneries at Home.................. 1 00
Moore, Rev. J. W. Orange Culture................... 1 00
My Vineyard at Lakeview 1.25
Origin of Cultivated Plants........................ 1 75
Parsons. On the Rose.............................. 1 50
Quinn. Pear Culture for Profit New and Revised Edition..... 1 00
Rivers. Miniature Fruit Garden 1 00
Rixford. Wine Press and Cellar....................... 1 50

Robinson. Ferns in their Homes and Ours.......................... 1.50
Roe. Success with Small Fruits................................... 5.00
Saunders. Insects Injurious to Fruits............................ 3.00
Sheehan, Jas. Your Plants. Paper.................................. .40
Stewart. Sorghum and Its Products................................ 1.50
Thomas. American Fruit Culturist................................. 2.00
Vick. Flower and Vegetable Garden. Cloth........................ 1.00
Warder. Hedges and Evergreens.................................... 1.50
Webb, Jas. Cape Cod Cranberries. Paper............................ .40
White. Cranberry Culture.. 1.25
Williams, B. S. Orchid Grower's Manual.......................... 6.50
Wood, Samuel. Modern Window Gardening........................... 1.25

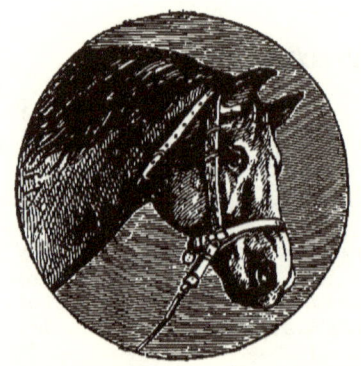 

Cattle, Dogs, Horses, Sheep, Swine, Poultry, Etc.

CATTLE, SHEEP, AND SWINE.

Allen, L. F. American Cattle. New and Revised Edition........... 2.50
Armatage, Prof. Geo. Every Man His Own Cattle Doctor. 8vo... 7.50
Armsby. Manual of Cattle Feeding................................ 2.50
Cattle. The Varieties, Breeding, and Management.................. .75
Coburn, F. D. Swine Husbandry. New and Revised Edition...... 1.75
Clok. Diseases of Sheep... 1.25
Dadd, Prof. Geo. H. American Cattle Doctor. 12mo............... 1.50
　　　　　　American Cattle Doctor. 8vo. Cloth...... 2.50
Fleming. Veterinary Obstetrics.................................. 6.00
Guenon. On Milch Cows... 1.00
Harris, Joseph. On the Pig...................................... 1.50
Jennings. On Cattle and their Diseases.......................... 1.25
　　　　　　On Sheep, Swine, and Poultry,........................... 1.25

O. JUDD CO.'S ALPHABETICAL CATALOGUE. 5

Jersey, Alderney, and Guernsey Cow 1.50
Keeping One Cow 1.00
Macdonald. Food from the Far West 1.50
McClure. Diseases of the American Horse, Cattle, and Sheep 2.00
McCombie, Wm. Cattle and Cattle Breeders 1.50
Martin, R. B. Hog-Raising and Pork-Making .... .40
Miles. Stock Breeding 1.50
Powers, Stephen. The American Merino for Wool and Mutton.
  A practical and valuable work 1.75
Quincy, Hon. Josiah. On Soiling Cattle 1.25
Randall. Fine Wool Sheep Husbandry 1.00
—— Practical Shepherd 2.00
—— Sheep Husbandry 1.50
Reasor. On the Hog 1.50
Sidney. On the Pig .... .50
Shepherd, Major W. Prairie Experience in Handling Cattle... 1.00
Stewart, Henry. Shepherd's Manual. New and Enlarged Edition.. 1.50
Stewart, E. W. Feeding Animals 2.00
The Sheep. Its Varieties and Management. Boards .... .75
Youatt and Martin. On the Hog 1.00
Youatt. On Sheep 1.00

DOGS, ETC.

Burgess. American Kennel and Sporting Field. 8vo 3.00
Dog—The Varieties and Management .... .50
Dogs of Great Britain, America, and Other Countries, Compiled from Stonehenge and other Standard Writers. The most Complete Work ever Published on the Dog. 12mo 2.00
Forester, F. The Dog, by Dinks, Mayhew, and Hutchinson. 8vo ... 3.00
Floyd, Wm. Hints on Dog Breaking. 12mo .... .50
Hallock, C. Dog Fanciers' Directory and Medical Guide. 18mo..... .25
Hammond, S. Dog Training. 12mo 1.00
Hill, J. W. Management and Diseases of the Dog. 12mo 2.00
Hooper, J. J. Dog and Gun. Paper .... .30
Hutchinson, G. N. Dog Breaking. 8vo 3.00
Idstone. The Dog. Illustrated. 12mo 1.25
Laverack, E. The Setter. 4to 3.00
Mayhew, E. Dogs; Their Management. 16mo .... .75
Points for Judging Different Varieties of Dogs.
  Paper .... .50
Richardson. Dogs; Their Origin and Varieties. Paper 30c. Cloth .60
Shaw, T. Vero. Illustrated Book of the Dog. 4to 8.00
Stables, Gordon. Our Friend the Dog. 8vo 3.00
—— Practical Kennel Guide 1.50
—— Ladies' Dogs as Companions 2.00

6   O. JUDD CO.'S ALPHABETICAL CATALOGUE.

Stonehenge. The Dog in Health and Disease. 8vo 3.00
——— Dogs of the British Islands. 8vo 6.00
——— The Greyhound 5.50
Youatt. On the Dog. 8vo 2.50

HORSES, RIDING, ETC.

Anderson, E. L. Modern Horsemanship. 8vo 7.00
——— The Gallop. 4to. Paper 1.00
Armatage, Geo. Every Man His Own Horse Doctor, together with Blaine's Veterinary Art. 8vo. ½ morocco 7.50
Armatage, Geo. Horse Owner and Stableman's Companion. 12mo 1.50
Battersby, Col. J. C. The Bridle Bits. A valuable little work on horsemanship. Fully illustrated. 12mo 1.00
Baucher, F. New Method of Horsemanship. 12mo 1.00
Bruce. Stud-Book. 4 vols 35.00
Chawner, R. Diseases of the Horse and How to Treat Them. 12mo 1.25
Chester. Complete Trotting and Pacing Record 10.00
Dadd, G. H. American Reformed Horse Book. 8vo 2.50
——— Modern Horse Doctor. 12mo 1.50
Day, W. The Race Horse in Training. 8vo 6.25
Du Hays, C. Percheron Horse. New and Revised Edition. 12mo. 1.00
Durant. Horseback Riding 1.25
Famous Horses of America. Cloth. 4to 1.50
Gleason, O. R. How to Handle and Educate Vicious Horses 1.00
Going, J. A. Veterinary Dictionary. 12mo 2.00
Herbert, H. W. Hints to Horse Keepers. 12mo 1.75
Helm, H. T. American Roadsters and Trotting Horses. 8vo 5.00
Horse, The; Its Varieties and Management. Boards .... .75
Howden, P. How to Buy and Sell the Horse. 12mo 1.00
Jennings, R. Horse Training Made Easy. 16mo 1.25
——— The Horse and His Diseases. 12mo 1.25
Law, J. Veterinary Adviser. 8vo 3.00
Liautard. Chart of Age of Domestic Animals .... .50
——— Animal Castration. 12mo 2.00
Manning. The Illustrated Stock Doctor 5.00
Mayhew, E. Illustrated Horse Management. 8vo 3.00
" Horse Doctor. 8vo 3.00
McClure, R. Diseases of American Horses. 12mo 2.00
——— American Gentleman's Stable Guide. 12mo 1.00
Miles, W. On the Horse's Foot. 12mo .... .75
Rarey. Horse Tamer and Farrier. 16mo .... .50
Riding and Driving .... .20
Riley, H. On the Mule. 12mo 1.50
Russell. Scientific Horse-Shoeing 1.00
Saddle Horse, The. Complete Guide to Riding and Training 1.00
Saunders. Horse Breeding. 12mo 2.00

O. JUDD CO.'S ALPHABETICAL CATALOGUE. 7

Stewart, R. American Farmer's Horse Book. 8vo 3.00
Stonehenge. Every Horse Owner's Cyclopædia. 8vo 3.75
——— On the Horse in the Stable and the Field. English Edition. 8vo 3.50
——— On the Horse in the Stable and the Field. American Edition. 12mo 2.00
Tellor. Diseases of Live Stock. Cloth, 2.50; Sheep 3.00
Wallace. American Stud-Book. Per vol 10.00
Williams. Veterinary Medicine 5.00
——— Veterinary Surgery 7.50
Woodruff. The Trotting Horse in America. 12mo.. .... 2.50
Woods, Rev. J. C. Horse and Man .... :................... 2.50
Youatt & Skinner. The Horse. 8vo 1.75
Youatt & Spooner. "   "   12mo....................... 1.50

———◆———

POULTRY AND BEES.

Burnham. New Poultry Book........... .... 1.50
Cook, Prof. A. J. Bee-Keeper's Guide or Manual of the Apiary.... 1.25
Cooper, Dr. J. W. Game Fowls..................................... 5.00
Corbett. Poultry Yard and Market. Paper................. .50
Felch, I. K. Poultry Culture...... .... 1.50
Halsted. Artificial Incubation and Incubators. Paper..... .... .75
Johnson, G. M. S. Practical Poultry Keeper. Paper........... .50
King. Bee-Keeper's Text Book.... ... . 1.00
Langstroth. On the Honey and Hive Bee................... 2.00
Poultry. Breeding, Rearing, Feeding etc. Boards .. .. .50
Profits in Poultry and their Profitable Management. Most complete Work extant..... .. .. 1.00
Quinby. Mysteries of Bee-Keeping Explained (Edited by L. C. Root). 1.50
Renwick. Thermostatic Incubator. Paper 36c. Cloth .... .56
Root, A. I. A, B, C, of Bee-Culture........ .... 1.25
Standard Excellence in Poultry............. .... 1.00
Stoddard. An Egg-Farm. Revised and Enlarged................... .50
Wright. Illustrated Book of Poultry............................. 8.00
——— Practical Poultry-Keeper..................... •............ 2.00
——— Practical Pigeon Keeper.. 1.50

Our Sportsman's Books

ANGLING, FISHING, ETC.

Burgess, J. T. Practical Guide to Bottom Fishing, Trolling, Spinning, Fly, and Sea Fishing. 8vo..................	.50
Fish Hatching and Fish Catching. By Roosevelt and Green. 12mo..	1.50
Forester, F. Fish and Fishing. New Edition. 8vo..................	2.50
—— Fishing with Hook and Line. Paper....................	.25
Fysshe and Fysshynge, from the Boke of St. Albans...........	1.00
Hamilton, M. D. Fly Fishing. 12mo...........................	1.75
Harris. The Scientific Angler—Foster..........................	1.50
Henshall, J. A. A Book of the Black Bass. 8vo.................	3.00
Keene, J. H. Fly-Fishing and Fly-Making. 12mo. Just Published..	1.50
—— Practical Fisherman. 12mo....................	4.00
King, J. L. Trouting on the Brulé River. 12mo...................	1.50
Norris, T. American Fish Culture. 12mo.......................	1.75
—— American Angler's Book. 8vo.......................	5.50
Orvis, Charles F. Fishing with the Fly. Crown 8vo...........	2.50
Pennell, H. C. Bottom; or, Float Fishing. Boards................	.50
—— Fly-Fishing and Worm-Fishing. Boards..........	.50
—— Trolling for Pike, Salmon, and Trout. Boards....	.50
Prime. I go a Fishing..	2.50
Random Casts, from an Angler's Note Book......	.50
Roosevelt, R. B. Game Fish of the Northern States and British Provinces. 12mo.	2.00
—— Superior Fishing; or, the Striped Bass, Trout, Black Bass, and Blue Fish of the Northern States. 12mo...........................	2.00

Roosevelt & Green. Fish Hatching and Fish Catching	1.50
Slack, J. H. Practical Trout Culture. 12mo	1.00
Scott, G. C. Fishing in American Waters. 8vo	2.50
Walton & Cotton. Complete Angler. 8vo	5.00
—— " " Bohn	2.00
—— " " Chandos	1.50
—— " " 12mo	.80

BOATING, CANOEING SAILING, ETC.

Canoeing in Kanuckia. 12mo	.75
Fellows, H. P. Boating Trips on New England Rivers. 12mo	1.25
Frazar, D. Practical Boat Sailing. 16mo	1.00
Henshall, J. A. Camping and Cruising in Florida. 12mo	1.50
Kemp, Dixon. Manual of Yacht and Boat Sailing (the Standard Authority). Royal 8vo. Illustrated	10.00
Kemp, Dixon. Yacht Designing. Folio	25.00
Kunhardt, D. T. Small Yachts. 4to, 14½ x 12½	7.00
Prescott, C. E. The Sailing Boat. 16mo	.50
Steele, T. S. Canoe and Camera. 12mo	1.50
Swimming. Routledge	.20

FIELD SPORTS AND NATURAL HISTORY.

American Bird Fancier. Enlarged edition	.50
Adams, H. G. Favorite Song Birds	1.50
Archer, Modern. Paper	.15
Bailey. Our Own Birds	1.50
Bird-Keeping. Fully Illustrated	1.50
Brown. Taxidermy	1.00
Canary Birds. New and Revised Edition. Paper, 50c. Cloth	.75
Coues. Key to North American Birds	10.00
Cocker. Manual	1.50
Edwards. Rabbits	1.25
Goode and Atwater. Menhaden	2.00
Holden. Book of Birds	.25
Lawn Tennis Hand Book	.75
Packard. Guide to Study of Insects	5.00
—— Half Hour Insects	2.50
—— Common Insects	1.50
Practical Rabbit Keeper	1.50
Swimming, Skating and Rinking	.25
Van Doren. Fishes of the East Atlantic Coast	1.50
Warne. Angling. Boards	.50
Wilson. American Ornithology. 3 vols	18.00
Wilson and Bonaparte. American Ornithology. 1 vol	7.00

HUNTING, SHOOTING, FISHING, ETC.

Adirondacks Guide. Wallace	2.00
Amateur Trapper. Boards	.75
Batty, J. H. How to Hunt and Trap. 12mo	1.50
—— Practical Taxidermy. 12mo	1.50
Barber. Crack Shot—the Rifleman's Guide. 12mo	1.25
Bogardus, Capt. Field, Cover, and Trap Shooting. 12mo	2.00
Bumstead. On the Wing	1.50
Dead Shot. A Treatise on the Gun	1.25
Farrow. How to Become a Crack Shot. 12mo	1.00
Forester, F. Life and Writings—D. W. Judd. 2 volumes. 8vo	3.00
—— Field Sports. 2 volumes. 8vo	4.00
—— Complete Manual for Young Sportsmen. 8vo	2.00
—— American Game in its Season. 8vo	1.50
Gildersleeve, H. A. Rifles and Marksmanship. 12mo	1.50
Gloan. The Breech-loader	1.25
Gould, J. M. How to Camp Out. 16mo	.75
Greener, W. W. Choke Bore Guns. 8vo	3.00
—— The Gun and its Development	2.50
Gun, Rod, and Saddle. "Ubique"	1.00
Hallock. Sportsman's Gazeteer and General Guide—A Treatise on all Game and Fish of North America. Instruction in Shooting, Fishing, Taxidermy, and Woodcraft, with Directory of Principal Game Resorts and Maps. New and Revised Edition. 12mo	3.00
Henderson, H. Practical Hints on Camping. 12mo	1.25
Lewis, E. J. The American Sportsman. 8vo	2.50
Murray. Adventures in the Wilderness. 12mo	1.25
Murphy, J. M. American Game Bird Shooting. 12mo	2.00
Newhouse. Trapper's Guide. 8vo	1.50
Pistol, The—How to Use. 12mo	.50
Prescott, C. E. Practical Hints on Rifle Practice with Military Arms	.50
Roosevelt, R. B. Florida, and the Game Water Birds of the Atlantic Coast and Lakes of the United States. 12mo	2.00
Samuels. Birds of New England and Adjacent States	4.00
Shooting on the Wing. 16mo	.75
Smith, George Putnam. The Law of Field Sports	1.00
Stonehenge. Rural Sports—The Standard Encyclopædia of Field Sports. ½ morocco. 8vo	5.00
Thrasher, H. Hunter and Trapper. 12mo	.75
Wingate, C. W. Manual for Rifle Practice. 16mo	1.50
Woodcraft. "Nessmuck." 12mo	1.00

ARCHITECTURE, ETC.

Allen, L. F. Rural Architecture 1.50
American Cottages... 5.00
Ames. Alphabets 1.50
Atwood. Country and Suburban Houses........................ 1 50
Barn Plans and Out-Buildings...................... 1.50
Bell. Carpentry Made Easy..................................... 5.00
Bicknell. Cottage and Villa Architecture...................... 4.00
——— Detail Cottage and Constructive Architecture............ 6.00
——— Modern Architectural Designs and Details................ 10.00
——— Public Buildings New.................................... 2.50
——— Street, Store, and Bank Fronts. New.................... 2.50
——— School-House and Church Architecture................... 2.50
——— Stables, Out-buildings, Fences, etc..................... 2.50
Brown. Building, Table and Estimate Book.................... 1.50
Burn. Drawing Books, Architectural. Illustrated and Ornamental.
3 Vols. Each... 1.00
Cameron. Plasterer's Manual................................... .75
Camp. How Can I Learn Architecture........................... .50
Copley. Plain and Ornamental Alphabets 8 00
Cottages. Hints on Economical Building...................... 1.00
Cummings. Architectural Details............................. 6.00
Elliott. Hand Book of Practical Landscape Gardening.......... 1.50
Eveleth. School-House Architecture.......................... 4.00
Fuller. Artistic Homes....................................... 3.50
Gilmore, Q. A. Roads and Street Pavements................... 2.50
Gould. American Stair-Builder's Guide....................... 2.50
——— Carpenter's and Builder's Assistant....................... 2.50
Hodgson. Steel Square 1.00
Holly. Art of Saw Filing .... .75
Harney. Barns, Out-Buildings, and Fences 4.00
Hulme. Mathematical Drawing Instruments.................... 1.50

12   O. JUDD CO.'S ALPHABETICAL CATALOGUE.

Hussey. Home Building.. 2.50
—— National Cottage Architecture. 4.00
Homes for Home Builders. Just Published. Fully Illustrated. 1.50
Interiors and Interior Details 7.50
Lakey. Village and Country Houses 5.00
Modern House Painting 5.00
Monckton. National Carpenter and Joiner 5.00
—— National Stair-Builder. 5.00
Painter, Gilder, and Varnisher's Companion 1.50
Palliser. American Cottage Homes. 3.00
—— Model Homes 1.00
—— Useful Details. 2.00
Plummer. Carpenters' and Builders' Guide .75
Powell. Foundations and Foundation Walls 2.00
Reed. Cottage Houses. 1.25
—— House Plans for Everybody. 1.50
—— Dwellings. 3.00
Riddell. Carpenter and Joiner Modernized 7.50
—— New Elements of Hand Railing. 7.00
—— Lessons on Hand Railing for Learners. 5.00
Rural Church Architecture 4.00
Scott. Beautiful Homes. 2.50
Tuthill. Practical Lessons in Architectural Drawing. 2.50
Weidenmann. Beautifying Country Homes. A superb quarto Vol. 10.00
Woodward. Cottages and Farm Houses. 1.00
—— Country Homes. 1.00
—— National Architect. Volumes 1 and 2. Each. 15.00
—— Suburban and Country Houses. 1.00

MISCELLANEOUS.

Collection of Ornaments 2.00
Common Sea Weeds. .50
Common Shells of the Seashore .50
Corson, Miss Juliet. Cooking School Text Book. 1.25
—— Twenty-five Cent Dinners. New Edition. .25
De Voe. Market Assistant. 2.50
Dussauce. On the Manufacture of Vinegar. 5.00
Eassie. Wood and its Uses. 1.50
Eggleston. Roxy 1.50
—— Circuit Rider. 1.50
—— School Boy. 1.00
—— Queer Stories. 1.00
—— End of the World 1.50
—— Mystery of Metropolisville. 1.50
—— Hoosier Schoolmaster.. 1.25
Elliott, Mrs. Housewife. New and Revised Edition. 1.25
Ewing. Hand Book of Agriculture. .25

O. JUDD CO.'S ALPHABETICAL CATALOGUE. 13

Ferns and Ferneries. Paper... .25
Fisher. Grain Tables. .40
Fowler. Twenty Years of Inside Life in Wall Street. 1.50
Gardner. Carriage Painters' Manual 1.00
—— How to Paint... 1.00
Hazard. Butter Making. .25
Household Conveniences 1.50
How to Detect the Adulterations of Food. Paper .25
How to Make Candy .50
Leary. Ready Reckoner .25
Myers. Havana Cigars. .25
Our Farmers' Account Book 1.00
Parloa, Miss. Cook Book. 1.50
Ropp. Commercial Calculator. .50
Scribner. Lumber and Log-Book. .35
Ware. The Sugar Beet. 4.00
Weston, J. Fresh Water Aquarium. Paper .25
Weir, Harrison. Every Day in the Country. .75
Wingate, Gen. G. W. Through the Yellowstone Park 1.50
Williams. Ladies' Fancy Work. 1.50
—— Evening Amusements. 1.50
—— Beautiful Homes 1.50
—— Ladies' Needle Work 1.00
—— Artistic Embroidery 1.00
Willard. Practical Butter Book. 1.00
—— Practical Dairy Husbandry 3.00
Warne's Useful Books. Boards. With practical Illustrations:
The Orchard and Fruit Garden. By ELIZABETH WATTS. .50
Vegetables and How to Grow Them. By ELIZABETH WATTS .50
Cattle and their Varieties. .50
The Dog and its Varieties. .50
Flowers and Flower Garden. By ELIZABETH WATTS. .50
Hardy Plants for Little Front Gardens. .50
Poultry—An Original and Practical Guide to their Management. .50
The Modern Fencer. By Capt. T. GRIFFITH. .50
The Modern Gymnast. By CHARLES SPENCER. .50
Cattle and their Varieties and Management. .75
The Horse and its Varieties and Management. .75
Sheep and its Varieties and Management. .75

Our Very Latest Publications.

Through the Yellowstone Park on Horseback. By Gen. G. W. Wingate..... 1.50
Fly-Fishing and Fly-Making. By Keene... 1.50
How to Handle and Educate Vicious Horses. By O. R. Gleason..... 1.00
The Law of Field Sports. By Geo. P. Smith........ 1.00
Bridle Bits. A Treatise on Practical Horsemanship. By Col. J. C. Battersby.. 1.00
The Percheron Horse in America and France.. 1.00
Profits in Poultry. Useful and Ornamental Breeds.. 1.00
Cape Cod Cranberries. By James Webb. Paper...... .50
How to Plant. By M. W. Johnson.............. .50
The American Merino for Wool and Mutton. By Stephen Powers...... 1.75

New and Revised Editions.

Hallock. Sportsman's Gazetteer........ 3.00
Stewart. Irrigation for the Farm, Garden and Orchard.. 1.50
Farm Implements and Machinery. By Thomas....... 1.50
Egg Farm. By Stoddard. Cloth.. .50
Play and Profit in My Garden.......... 1.50
Silos and Ensilage .... .50

Send Postal for Complete Catalogue of our Publications regarding Horses and Horsemanship, Hunting, Fishing, and all other Out-Door Sports and Pastimes.

O. JUDD CO., DAVID W. JUDD, Pres't.
751 BROADWAY, NEW YORK.

JUST PUBLISHED.

THE BEST BOOK ON GARDENING EVER WRITTEN.
Gardening for Profit.

A Guide to the Successful Culture of the Market and Family Garden.

PROFUSELY ILLUSTRATED.

Entirely Rewritten and Greatly Enlarged.

By PETER HENDERSON,

Author of "Practical Floriculture," "Gardening for Pleasure," "Garden and Farm Topics," etc.

The immense and unprecedented sale of the earlier editions of Mr. Henderson's book, "Gardening for Profit," which sale has been continuous since the first day of its issue, indicates the estimate of its value as a thoroughly practical work. The new book, just issued, contains the best of the former work, with large additions drawn from the author's added years of experience. It cannot but be regarded by all as the best work on Market and Family Gardening ever published.

Cloth, 12mo. Price, Post-paid, $2.00.

O. JUDD CO., DAVID W. JUDD, Pres't, 751 Broadway, N. Y.

The ✣ American ✣ Agriculturist.
➤ FOR THE ◄
Farm, Garden and Household.
Established in 1842.
The Best and Cheapest Agricultural Journal in the World.

 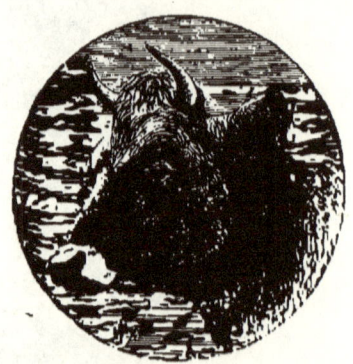

The *American Agriculturist* (so-called because started in 1842, as a Rural Periodical) has been greatly enlarged and widened in scope, without change of name, until it now meets the wants of ALL classes, in City, Village and Country; it is literally EVERYBODY'S PAPER. It helps the FARMER, the GARDENER, the FRUIT GROWER, the MECHANIC, the PROFESSIONAL and BUSINESS man; it greatly aids every HOUSEKEEPER; it pleases and instructs the YOUTH and the LITTLE ONES.

It is edited with **great care**, labor, and expense, to have every line reliable, while its pages abound in a great variety of **useful, practical, reliable information** and suggestions.

Every number describes, with engravings, a great variety of Labor-saving, Labor-helping devices and Household Economies, Animals, Plants, Flowers, etc. In this respect it surpasses, by far, all other like journals, and will be found valuable and helpful by every one, no matter how many other journals he may have.

Its constant **Exposures** of **Humbugs** and Swindling Schemes are invaluable everywhere, and save many times its cost to almost every reader. It admits no medical advertisements, and no untrustworthy advertisers. Its large circulation enables the Publishers to issue it at very low rates, and to deal liberally with subscribers in the way of premiums, etc.

TERMS, which include postage *pre-paid* by the Publishers: $1.50 per annum, in advance; 3 copies for $4; 4 copies for $5; 5 copies for $6; 6 copies for $7; 7 copies for $8; 10 or more copies, only $1 each. Single Numbers, 15 cents.

➤✣ AMERIKANISCHER ✣ AGRICULTURIST. ✣◄

The only purely Agricultural German paper in the United States, and the best in the world. It contains all the principal matter of the English Edition, together with special departments for German cultivators, prepared by writers trained for the work. Terms same as for the *American Agriculturist*.

O. JUDD CO., DAVID W. JUDD, Pres't, 751 Broadway, N. Y.

www.ingramcontent.com/pod-product-compliance
Lightning Source LLC
Chambersburg PA
CBHW031951230426

43672CB00010B/2122